SOLIDARITY
WITH CHILDREN

An Essay Against Adult Supremacy

Madeline Lane-McKinley

Haymarket Books
Chicago, IL

Published in 2025 by
Haymarket Books
P.O. Box 180165
Chicago, IL 60618
773-583-7884
www.haymarketbooks.org
info@haymarketbooks.org

ISBN: 979-8-88890-465-7

Distributed to the trade in the US through Consortium Book Sales
and Distribution (www.cbsd.com) and internationally through In-
gram Publisher Services International (www.ingramcontent.com).

This book was published with the generous support of Lannan Foundation, Wallace Action Fund, and the Marguerite Casey Foundation.

Special discounts are available for bulk purchases by organizations
and institutions. Please email info@haymarketbooks.org for more
information.

Cover design by Rachel Cohen.

Printed in Canada by union labor.

Library of Congress Cataloging-in-Publication data is available.
Library of Congress Control Number: 2025943396

12

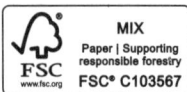

Praise for *Solidarity with Children*

"In a world that weaponizes the ideal of childhood, not least against children themselves, Lane-McKinley reveals how adult supremacy inflicts violence—from genocidal colonialism to the repressive halls of school. Rejecting mere protection and unsettling the bounds of childhood and adulthood, this book is a demand for a revolutionary solidarity with children through building a world of communal care. It draws on past and present activism to illuminate the radical politics that would empower children to become political subjects capable of mounting struggles in a world of climate catastrophe, economic crisis, and global war. Unflinching and visionary, *Solidarity with Children* is an indispensable guide for anyone committed to transforming the world."

—**Anne Boyer**, author of *The Undying: A Meditation on Modern Illness*

"This extraordinary book changed me, and still reverberates in my mind. Its stunning, clear-eyed, breathtaking clarity is a call to arms for us all."

—**Noreen Masud**, author of *A Flat Place: Moving Through Empty Landscapes, Naming Complex Trauma*

"As a sixty-something-year-old former child who knew I was trans but couldn't do anything about it back then, I'm proud to stand in solidarity with young people today who still need emancipation from a social construction of childhood that denies their agency and ability to know their own best interests. Madeline Lane-McKinley's important book makes clear just how high the stakes are."

—**Susan Stryker**, author of *Transgender History: The Roots of Today's Revolution*

For those who once were
or continue to be children
& let that be all of us.

Contents

A World Against Children

A few weeks after I began writing this book, Israel declared war on Gaza, following a series of attacks by Hamas and other militants on October 7, 2023. "We are fighting *human animals*, and we act accordingly," pronounced Israel's then minister of defense, Yoav Gallant, ordering a complete siege of the Gaza Strip.[1] At the time, half of the 2.2 million people living in the open-air prison of Gaza were under the age of fifteen. So many of these children, all born under siege, have since been massacred by the Israeli military, along with so many of their elders.

That October, much of what we witnessed in this genocide came as images of suffering children: a constant stream of photographs of children screaming, crying, fleeing, bloodied, injured, dead. One of the most enduring images of the first weeks was captured by photographer Mohammad Salem in a hospital in the southern Gaza Strip, where Inas Abu Maamar embraced the corpse of her five-year-old niece Saly, wrapped in a shroud and balanced on her knee.[2]

Days later, another image, taken by photographer Mahmud Hams, incited controversy: it depicted six small children lying in a row, covered in dried blood beneath a white sheet in the morgue of Al-Aqsa Hospital in the central Gaza Strip. Yet the image was deemed too "graphic" to be circulated by mainstream media outlets. The *New York Times* decided not to publish the photograph in full, instead using a cropped version to accompany a column.[3] Of this decision, *Times* Opinion editor Kathleen Kingsbury explained, "As editors, we ask a series of questions before publishing sensitive photos," such as: "Does the image respect the dignity of the victims? Is it exploitative or gratuitous? . . . Does the image help describe the news event in a way that has more impact than reporting alone can do?"[4] That same day, the *Times* published a column by former *Huffington Post* editor in chief Lydia Polgreen, who argued against this editorial decision, stating that it is "an image that demands to be seen." To this we might add, what does it mean to *see* this image? And what does it mean to crop it? In the version featured in the *Times*, the children's faces are left out of view: "If you don't look too closely," Polgreen writes, "you might think the photograph is a dimly lit snapshot from a slumber party or a family camping trip."[5] You would not know, for instance, that the child second from the left appears to be missing a chunk of their skull.

That fall, disputes erupted everywhere over photographs and videos. One of the key points of contention was whether these images were of Israeli children or of Palestinian children. And there were copious rumors and conspiracies, such as the notion that the children depicted were not *real* but in fact plastic dolls. Soon a story began to disseminate about forty Israeli children believed to have been beheaded by Hamas in the Be'eri kibbutz, which political leaders across the world quickly corroborated. In a statement that made headlines across the US media, President Joe Biden claimed, "I never really thought that I would see, have confirmed, pictures of terrorists beheading children." But soon the White House walked back this statement.[6] When journalists attempted to substantiate the story, which was reported by Israeli soldiers, the Israel Defense Forces (IDF) refused.[7] Meanwhile, the notion of these forty decapitated Israeli children, precisely as figures of innocence, was used relentlessly to justify the massacre of Palestinians, including children. "We will not allow a reality in which Israeli children are murdered," Yoav Gallant told the press, just as the death toll in Gaza surpassed a thousand.[8]

Nearly everywhere in this horror are traces of a political question: Which children get to be innocent—and which children are merely *human animals*? Appeals to innocence "demarcate who is killable," as poet and scholar Jackie Wang writes, "even if we are trying to strategically use such appeals to protest violence."[9] In the unbearable context of Gaza, we see variations on the figure of the child put into conflict with each other. Children's innocence, at a rhetorical level, legitimates genocide by the Israeli state and, conversely, stands in for the innocence of all Palestinians living under apartheid, whether they are children or adults, and no matter what form their resistance to their oppression has taken. At the heart of this innocence is a conception of children as something *like* human animals: as not-quite-humans and not-quite–historical subjects. As innocent, the child is likewise imagined as being without agency. In this sense, the story of decapitated children found by Israeli soldiers, made into the mouthpieces of Israel's attack on nearly a million children in Gaza, is even more devastating.

I want to ask the question again: Which children get to be innocent? Said another way, which children get to be seen *as children*?

Here, my thoughts turn to Tamir Rice, murdered at the age of twelve by the police in Cleveland, Ohio, in November 2014. He was holding a toy gun in a playground when officer Timothy Loehmann shot him upon arrival. I think of Aiyana Jones, who was murdered in May 2010 by police during a raid of the wrong apartment in Detroit, Michigan. She was seven years old. When the police shot her, she was asleep on the couch of an apartment she shared with her mother and grandmother. I think of Aderrien Murry, an eleven-year-old boy who was shot in the chest by a police officer, after he called 9-1-1 for help at his home in Indianola, Mississippi, in May 2023. His mother had asked him to make the call. Unlike Rice and Jones, Murry survived. I think of countless others: children who've been murdered and harmed, children who live in fear of state violence. Black children are six times more likely than white children to be shot by police in the United States.[10] Black children, in this sense, don't get to be children—Tamir Rice didn't get to be a child playing with a toy in a playground.

And part of the reason some children are not seen as children is that they are not seen *as humans*. Rather, even the most privileged children are imagined as property. It was by this logic that in May 2018, Attorney General Jeff Sessions spoke of migrant children being "smuggled" over the border, like bags of cocaine. In order to rationalize the horrors of family separation at the US–Mexico border, Sessions said, "If you are smuggling a child then we will prosecute you, and that child will be separated from you as required by law."[11] Between April 19 and May 31 that year, the Department of Homeland Security later acknowledged separating nearly two thousand children from parents or legal guardians at the border.[12] Of those children, hundreds were taken from their caretakers. Like many, I won't forget reading the story told by a human rights advocate who observed a caged teenager teaching children how to change the diapers of infants and toddlers who'd been separated from family members.[13]

That June, images of children in cages became emblematic of a rising fascism under the presidency of Donald Trump, even as the cages themselves were constructed during the Obama administration, and family separations never stopped under the Biden administration.[14] These images were from places like the repurposed warehouse in McAllen, Texas, where about fifteen hundred children were caged behind metal fences under nonstop overhead lighting, with only large pieces of foil to use as blankets and little food or water. While bringing attention to this crisis at the border, these images of horrific dehumanization are also horrifically dehumanizing. The faces of the children can't be fully seen: they are blurry and out of focus. They can be reduced to symbols of innocence, just as they can be reduced to that which can be "smuggled" and therefore confiscated by the state. It was out of the attempt to humanize these children locked in cages at the border that they also became figures of the inhumane.

"To photograph is to appropriate the thing photographed," as Susan Sontag warned us, writing at the end of the Vietnam War.[15] Images can transfix, and anesthetize, sometimes despite our best intentions: "To suffer is one thing," she wrote, "another thing is living with the photographed images of suffering, which does not necessarily strengthen conscience and the ability to be compassionate. It can also corrupt them. Once one has seen such images, one has started down the road of seeing more."[16] In December 2023, two months into the Israeli airstrikes, scholar and author Steven Salaita described a new version of this phenomenon as "scrolling through genocide." We are the first generation to witness genocide in real time, as Salaita writes: "History books about the horrors of the past are written every time somebody opens social media."[17]

Twenty-six years after she published her 1977 essay collection *On Photography*, as the Iraq War began (and soon before her death), Sontag penned an addendum, *Regarding the Pain of Others*. "To those who are sure that right is on one side, oppression and injustice on the other," Sontag writes, "what matters is precisely who is killed by whom." All photographs "wait to be explained or falsified by their captions," she argues, recalling a familiar story: "During the fighting between Serbs and Croats at the beginning of the recent Balkan wars, the same photographs of children killed in the shelling of a village were passed around at both Serb and Croat propaganda briefings. Alter the caption, and the children's deaths could be used and reused."[18] To this end, she suggests that the case against war "does not rely on information about who and when and where"—to the contrary, "the arbitrariness of the relentless slaughter is evidence enough."[19]

When the IDF began propagating the story of the forty Israeli children allegedly beheaded by Hamas, there were immediate demands for photographic evidence. Days later, media outlets in the US that had contributed to the circulation of this claim began reporting instead that it was unsubstantiated. At that point, however, it was too late: what had been stoked in the political imagination could not be undone. The idea of these forty children continued to serve as a justification for Israel's obliteration of Gaza. At the time the story was rescinded, more than two thousand four hundred Palestinian children had already been killed by Israel—an annual record since the year 2000. Then, within a week, the Israeli military killed one thousand thirty more Palestinian children in Gaza. This is a figure that bears repeating: one thousand thirty more children were massacred in a matter of days. It's difficult not to set that number against the other—to reduce these lives to body counts, as if measuring a genocide could make it somehow more perceivable *as a genocide*. The body counts become like the ongoing circulation of images, seeming to prove, over and over again, the existence of what nevertheless goes unrecognized.

In this paradigm of scrolling through genocide, such images of suffering children "bring with them the inevitability of more to come, a grotesque production line of suffering on view," as writer Yasmin El-Rifae suggests. While the only reasonable response may be shock and rage, El-Rifae asks how we can avoid the ways this rage ossifies into feelings of guilt or shame, "which uselessly burrow inwards."[20] A part of this means learning to look at these feelings. And perhaps, in learning to look at the pain of these images, we might learn to unmake the world that has made this pain not only possible but supposedly inevitable. This is merely how the world works, too many will tell you—imagining otherwise would be *childish*. To this charge, I hope this book can provide a useful retort.

§

Throughout the fall of 2023, I was reminded of the fall of 2001. That was the moment of my own political awakening, and perhaps also the end of my childhood. More than as a loss of innocence, I remember the period immediately following September 11 as a time of both intense radicalization and political disappointment. My friends and I watched the second plane hit the World Trade Center on the television sets that teachers had wheeled into our high school classrooms, and weeks later, we protested the bombing of Afghanistan. We ditched school, and we didn't tell our parents. We left after lunch period and drove to a demonstration held at the University of New Mexico campus. At some point we moved off campus and onto Central Avenue, one of the main arteries of Albuquerque, where police lined the sidewalks and eventually broke up the crowd by force.

My best friend and I fled, heading back to her house, feeling powerless in the face of repression but also like we were living in history, doing something like our parents had when they stood up to the Vietnam War.

But when I told my father about it later that night, he was hardly proud of me. He said that I didn't understand the complexity of the situation. He explained that "we" had to defend ourselves against terrorism, insisting that there were no other options. So many people would come to have regrets about that time. Most of my friends found themselves in conflict with parents, grandparents, and other members of the adult world. About a decade later, my father apologized for his reaction. He was better than most in this regard, which I don't fail to appreciate. At the time, though, I remember feeling that he thought I'd been foolish—that I'd acted childishly.

On the left, the charge of "childish" politics has a long history. In 1920, Vladimir Lenin notoriously denounced critics of the Bolsheviks as part of the "infantile disorder" of left communism. Describing this "very young trend," Lenin concluded that "under certain conditions, the disease can be easily eradicated, and we must set to work with the utmost energy to eradicate it."[21] Using similar terms, Mao Zedong condemned political "adventurism": "Some regard their fantasies as truth, while others strain to realize in the present an ideal which can only be realized in the future," he argued. "They alienate themselves from the current practice of the majority of people and from the realities of the day, and show themselves adventurist in their actions."[22] In his widely translated 1880 pamphlet *Socialism:*

Utopian and Scientific, Friedrich Engels, too, mobilized these tropes in his critique of the idealism of utopian socialism. The pejorative use of "utopia" was instrumental to legitimating Marxism, by contrast, as a scientific method. And among anarchists, themselves often the target of this rhetoric of childishness and idealism, there is also a tradition of such claims—as in Murray Bookchin's influential critique of "lifestyle anarchism" in the 1990s, based on the lifestylist's "petulantly infantile ego that ostensibly precedes history."[23] In the 1960s, the New Left performed an inversion of this adultist logic: the famous refrain "Don't Trust Anyone over Thirty," coined by activist Jack Weinberg in 1964, was part of the Berkeley Free Speech Movement.[24] But of course, among that generation of leftists, now well beyond their thirties, far too many bemoan the supposed "wokeness" and "mob mentality" of today's youth, what some call the "snowflake generation." Within the left, this language of infantilization is consistently employed to demarcate what and who has gone *too far*, too often for the sake of defending the status quo, if not to moralize reformism.

But what would the left be without such ongoing tensions in the struggle toward social transformation? What remains of this idea of "the left" without the call, which spread through the streets of Paris during the global uprisings of 1968, to *be realistic: demand the impossible!*? What is lost when we limit our political horizons to what is supposedly "realistic"? And who gets to decide what can and can't be possible?

These questions were echoed in an open letter written by youth climate activists in 2020: "Doing your best is no longer

good enough. . . . You must now do the seemingly impossible."
The statement from Climate Emergency EU reverses the rhetoric and logic of political maturity and realism:

> Even a child can see that the climate and ecological
> crisis cannot be solved within today's system. . . . And
> even though you might have the option of ignoring the
> climate crisis, that is not an option for us—for your
> children. Right now, there is no place on earth where
> children face a future in a safe environment. This is
> and will be very much a reality for the rest of our lives.
> We ask you to face the climate emergency.[25]

As they argue, facing the reality of this crisis means thinking beyond our current systems. In this sense, the statement's emphasis on the *seemingly* impossible is utterly crucial.

In many ways, youth climate activists' call for a fully decarbonized economy is a utopian demand, what Marxist-feminist scholar Kathi Weeks characterizes as "a political demand that takes the form not of a narrowly pragmatic reform but of a more substantial transformation of the present configuration of social relations." A utopian demand is a demand "that raises eyebrows," as Weeks explains, "one for which we would probably not expect immediate success." Importantly, it is not impossible to achieve; it is merely constrained by our present reality.[26] The utopian demand asks the question of what we perceive as feasible, against the reality of what we know to be urgent. The utopian demand is not, in fact, strictly utopian in the sense of a "no place" to be dreamed up and mapped. To the contrary, it is grounded in reality, taking into account all its hellishness. What makes a demand specifically *utopian*, Weeks argues, is the way it prefigures a different world.

The attempt to even slow down the global climate crisis requires of us this awareness, however faint, that a different world is possible. What is perhaps most disturbing about having witnessed this crisis worsen so exponentially over the last few decades is that so many people are only acknowledging its reality now that it is supposedly "too late." The bravest position, it might seem, is to face our doom and to plan for it, as if nothing else can be done. This is just the way it is. As some contend, this is the way *it has to be.* Yet we are already living in an unimaginable world. We speak of what is and isn't "realistic" in a reality we cannot bear.

This book demands that we learn to act in solidarity with children. Doing so involves first reckoning with our own sense of possibility, and meeting the challenge posed by youth climate activists: that we stop "pretending that empty words will make the emergency go away," and bring to an end the arrogance that enables this belief. We cannot allow ourselves or each other to surrender the future.

§

At the center of this book is a claim that we live in a world that is profoundly against children. What I am describing is not a hatred of children, though hatred of children is certainly an aspect of it. Even in its idealization of children, this world is against children. While it may idealize *some* children, it harms *all* children—it is a world that, day by day, renders their future more apocalyptic, and in which they are taught, day by day, that this is just inevitable. We make this hell normal, knowing that children will most likely live out something far worse, the terror of which we can only begin to recognize.

Of course, most of the time, for adults who spend time with children, this reality must be kept out of the foreground. It's too painful to think about while caring for young people who need you to not be crying all the time. But this reality is everywhere: it is inescapable. It is the reality of Palestinian and Israeli children, whose violent deaths are weighed against each other; the reality of children as young as five years old working with bare hands in the cobalt mines of the Democratic Republic of Congo; the reality of over 330 million children living in extreme poverty worldwide;[27] the reality of the immigrant children caged at borders, of the trans children targeted by the state, of the one in three Black and Latinx households with children in the US facing food insecurity, and of the roughly one billion children worldwide who experience physical, sexual, or emotional violence each year.[28]

Five days a week, the person I love most in this world is in a public school classroom in a country where school shootings are rampant and increasing by the year. There simply aren't days when the thought doesn't hang over teachers and staff in schools, or days when children, parents, guardians, and caretakers are not constantly reminded of this possibility. In 2018, 113 people were killed or injured in school shootings in the

US. On average, there was a shooting once every eight school days that year—the worst on record, until soon it was not.[29] That March, youth activists against gun violence organized the March for Our Lives in Washington, DC. Delaney Tarr, the activist and Parkland shooting survivor who cofounded March for Our Lives, remembers a particular slogan, spread across signs at the event: "The Kids Will Save Us." In a 2022 essay for *Teen Vogue*, Tarr shared her frustrations with this slogan and what she describes as the "youth activist industrial complex." "The Kids Will Save Us" followed the activists for years. With each shooting, Tarr recalls feeling a sense of guilt and failure, precisely "because we were 'the kids,' but we hadn't saved them." At the same time, she explains, "nobody ever asked *how* are the kids supposed to save us."[30]

If children are imagined as having any agency at all in this world, they are delegated with the impossible task of saving the planet. In this effort, youth are encouraged to focus on legislative demands—doing work for votes, in a system in which children have no right to vote. This was certainly the case for March for Our Lives, which itself demobilized autonomous organizing among high school students for a nationwide strike and reoriented their energy toward gun control laws.

For the religious right, this world against children is most clearly illuminated by what is done in the name of children. Take the nonprofit organization Moms for Liberty, whose stated mission is to "promote liberty" and "fight for our children." The organization describes itself as dedicated to the "survival of America" through "unifying, educating and empowering parents to defend their parental rights at all levels of government."[31] This notion of "liberty" has nothing to do with child liberation or children's rights, but takes the form of parental rights and ownership over children—as well as discrimination against minoritized children for the sake of implicitly white, gender-normative, and therein *innocent* children. The most significant accomplishment of the group has been to mobilize book bans and curricular bans in public education on subjects such as slavery, racism, and LGBTQ history. Made on behalf of "liberty-minded" families and their children, these calls for school censorship are inconspicuous attacks on non-white and queer children. They have been instrumental to a broader culture of adult parental rights "activists" harassing, abusing, and endangering trans and nonbinary children and their caretakers, including parents and educators.

Certain stories are becoming more familiar to our times, like that of a man forcibly removed from a fourth-grade track meet in Kelowna, British Columbia, after he accosted a nine-year-old and demanded proof that she was female, as his wife screamed and called the child's parents "genital mutilators."[32] Or the story of an anti–Pride Day rally held at Saticoy Elementary in North Hollywood, where violence erupted after more than a hundred parents formed to chant antigay slurs as a hundred or so counterprotesters formed a human chain around the school to protect LGBTQ children and families.[33] Along with such direct attacks on children by adults, the "parental rights" phenomenon has exacerbated bullying at school and on social media among children, worsened the learning conditions and safety of many students, and most certainly contributed to the increase of youth suicide and suicidal ideation, which has doubled in the last decade.[34]

Anti-abortion politics operate by this same logic: fetishizing the *idea* of the innocent child (the fetus), while failing to care for *real* children. While insisting that inclusive public school education is "government overreach," the Christian right promotes state authoritarianism when it comes to all matters of reproductive health, exerting control over people's bodily autonomy that results in harm to both fetus and gestator. In the US, the pregnancy-related mortality rate has doubled over the last two decades, with Black and Indigenous women facing disproportionately high risks.[35] But the anti-child politics of the "pro-life" agenda are thrown into starker relief on the topic of youth access to abortion. Adolescents are most impacted by post-*Roe* state restrictions and experience the most barriers to seeking safe and legal abortions, including state requirements of parental consent. Due to delays in care, youth pregnancies face greater risk of medical complications as well.[36] In the name of children, this is violence *against children*. We shouldn't need to hear about the worst-case scenarios—like the ten-year-old incest victim in Ohio who was forced to travel out of state for an abortion, or the thirteen-year-old rape victim who gave birth after being denied an abortion in Mississippi—to know that all forcible pregnancies and forcible childbirths are the products of sexual violence.[37] This can be—and *needs* to be—a site of shared struggle for adults and children.

Recognition of the ways our struggles are shared is fundamental to building solidarity with children. As child liberationist writer carla joy bergman suggests, "Part of trusting and listening to kids is being open to what the path forward can and will look like with them."[38] For so many adults, this may feel impossible. To think about the future at all—whether in apocalyptic, denialist, or revolutionary terms—presents a daily challenge. But these are the stakes of solidarity with children: to take collective responsibility for our future, whatever it may be. This is also a matter of following the lead of youth movements. Across calls for a Free Gaza, protests against raids by Immigration and Customs Enforcement (ICE) and police violence, demands for access to abortions and gender-affirming care, and the fight against global climate crisis, youth today are at the forefront of our most urgent political struggles. None of this is new. Whether as a talisman for hope or as a mere scapegoat for generational conflicts, the role of youth has, time and again, been overlooked—or worse, overwritten. We owe it to each other to show up together, in as many ways as possible.

Among leftists today, the primary challenge of acting in political solidarity with children lies in circumnavigating the false binary of parental versus state rights, which is premised on the absence—and unthinkability—of children's rights. Wherever there are political conflicts over children, this authoritarian opposition looms. According to the logic of "parental rights," the child is conceived exclusively as the private property of the family. Of course, these rights do not extend to the parents and legal guardians of LGBTQ youth, whose parental rights have been targeted by the state—in Texas, for instance, Governor Greg Abbott called on the state's Department of Family and

Protective Services to undertake a "prompt and thorough in-vestigation" of reported gender-affirming care of youth, which he claimed "can legally constitute child abuse under several provisions."[39] To combat this terror, often out of desperation, we too fall back on the logic of parental rights and ownership over children: there are no other clear means to protect them. As any adult committed to supporting a child against these forces is well aware, nearly half of LGBTQ youth consider sui-cide each year. If they are fortunate enough to have parents and legal guardians who trust them—or who even *try* to trust them—they have a far better chance to survive into adulthood. Meanwhile, many queer youth live in fear of their parents and the state alike, even as they struggle against stigma and bully-ing at school.

The fascist turn of recent years has made political solidar-ity with children increasingly dangerous work. In this time, the trans child, as a figure of child autonomy, has posed what would seem the ultimate threat to the social order—hence the second Trump administration's immediate assault on trans children and their families upon inauguration. Throughout the twentieth century, trans children have been rendered what historian Jules Gill-Peterson articulates as a "problem of plas-ticity, rather than recognizing their personhood."[40] Under this logic, she explains, modern medicine reduces children's bodies to "their unfinishedness and plastic potential to be changed as they grow."[41] The capacity to change and be changed is at the heart of contemporary moral panic over "grooming" and trans children, wherein "reading to children, speaking to children, even speaking about children have all been brandished as evidence [of] predation," as writer Max Fox observes.[42] Since I began writing about these issues, I have grown used to harassment on the internet, including death threats. However, there is no way to grow used to the targeting of the child I care for. So often framed as concern for the child's well-being, this targeting includes inquiries about their genitalia by fascists who toss off accusations of pedophilia at anyone who speaks up in solidarity with trans children. "Irony" is not a strong enough word for this fascist obsession with the bodies of children. Parenting and caretaking for trans and nonbinary youth is riddled with uncertainties about safety every day: whether and how to keep "stealth," as we describe living-in-hiding in schools and other child-centered spaces, where harassment and violence are likely; how to advocate without violating the children we care for; how to help children find ways to survive under such conditions of adult supremacy.

Especially for non-white children, navigating the potential for violence is fundamental to parenting and caretaking; it is a mothering that, as Claudia Rankine writes, "remains as precarious as ever."[43] In an essay published after the 2015 Charleston church massacre, Rankine recalls asking a friend what it's like to be the mother of a Black son: "'The condition of black life is one of mourning,' she said bluntly. For her, mourning lived in real time inside her and her son's reality: at any moment she might lose her reason for living."[44] Of this maternal condition of mourning, author and activist Trina Greene Brown speaks to the "harm-reduction techniques" of Black parenting, shaped by police violence and surveillance, such as "not allowing my children to speak up for fear of them being considered a threat; having 'the talk' with my children on how to engage with police; being the 'fashion police' for fear that what my child is wearing could cause deadly interaction with the police." What is a parent or caretaker to do? Thinking through this as a child liberationist question, Brown reflects on the ways that parenting within these restrictions so easily slips into dominance over children. "I was parenting to protect," she explains, "but protection did not allow my child to be free."[45]

How do we imagine a political movement that's not "for the children" but actually *with* children and *for* our future? How can we make this imaginable not just in the abstract but in our everyday lives, in the ways we treat each other, make decisions together, and listen?

These questions stormed through my mind in early September 2020, as a nearby wildfire in southern Oregon was gaining force. My partner and kid and I decided to pack our cat and dog and a few suitcases in the car and evacuate our house. That day, the winds happened to be moving away from us, eventually spreading the fire to several towns within a matter of hours. We were made to feel "lucky" in the midst of a devastating catastrophe. Four people died in the fire, and about 2,600 homes burned down to the ground. It remains, at the time when I write this, the most destructive wildfire in the state's history. Those who were most impacted were doubly vulnerable: many who were displaced by the fire were also undocumented and living away from their communities of origin as agricultural workers in the Rogue Valley. As undocumented workers, many were unbanked and reported losing sizable savings that were held in cash in their burned homes, and were deemed ineligible for federal disaster relief after the fires. As we learned of the aftermath in the days that followed, I wondered how to talk about this, as a parent to a then eight-year-old child. We could say simple things like "this is scary," though even that felt difficult. What should I tell this incredibly perceptive, often introspective young person? Or, more importantly, what should I ask them about what they were experiencing and perceiving? And how should I ask?

Earlier that year, I found myself similarly conflicted, as we learned to talk about the COVID-19 pandemic, adapted to life "sheltering in place," and, later, developed shared agreements about public masking and potential exposure. We tried to do this as collaboratively as possible. At the same time, my partner and I struggled to put the idea of collective decision-making into practice, and to weigh the value of shared decisions against the desire for our child to feel cared for, and loved, under the apocalyptic conditions we'd brought them into. I have to wonder what this world will look like in 2029, the year when they will reach "adulthood." I often find myself with this thought at night, feeling terribly awake.

We are all born into a world that we never asked for. This is my reply to Adrienne Rich, who declares at the outset of her classic feminist text *Of Woman Born* that "the one unifying, incontrovertible experience shared by all women and men is that months-long period we spent unfolding inside a woman's body," and that "all human life on the planet is born of woman."[46] Far more compelling than Rich's essentialist conception of "woman"—which many have since rightly troubled—is the idea of children at the core of her statement. That is: we were all brought here without our consent. As adults and children, as humans, we have this in common. That's what it means to be born and to survive. We never asked for this world, and yet each day we wake up a part of it, and we participate in re-creating it. We might help it to continue, or we might do our best to sabotage it. But we are all a part of it.

§

On November 7, 2023, a group of about two dozen Palestinian children held a press conference outside what was once the Al-Shifa Hospital in Gaza, before it was raided and destroyed by Israel. A ten-year-old boy acted as the group's spokesperson: "We came to shout as children, urging you all to protect us. Stop the death. We want life. We want peace," he declared. "We want medicine. We want food. We want education. We want life."[47] There were echoes around the world. Later that week, at a youth-organized rally outside Seattle, a demand—Kids Say: Stop Bombing Kids!—cut through so much at the time, including the flurry of political rhetoric over *which* children and *whose* children. In these calls for solidarity from and by children, we are confronted by the ways children are instrumentalized without being heard. Solidarity with children can never be possible without listening to children.

Much of this book is written against children *as an idea*. For this reason, the figure of the fetus will hardly appear, nor will any natalist debates about whether to "bring children into this world." Rather, the starting point is that children have been brought into this world already, not as ideas but as human beings. What follows is an interrogation of some of the fantasy structures about children that stand in the way of making solidarity thinkable, and that legitimate forms of domination. These fantasies include the fetishization of children as innocent and the degradation of children as naive and undeserving of rights, along with the long history of Western imperialism's conceptualization of the child as the Other—the "uncivilized" who must be subjugated. At stake in the figure of the child is the question of what it means to be human. This is the question underlying Yoav Gallant's description of Palestinians as "human animals," and which writer Nadia Bou Ali rearticulates as a lesson: the children of Gaza today, she writes, "speak for the very concept of the living."[48]

In seeking to imagine solidarity with children, this is not a call to *protect* children, as many on the left have framed as a demand, nor is it a call to *save* the children, as the late antigay crusader Anita Bryant put it. It also isn't a call to simply *include* children, as if inclusion doesn't just amount to a different kind of marginalization. It is a call for solidarity, which demands a thorough dismantling of the premise of adult power in these logics of protecting, saving, and including children, replacing them with more rigorous forms of political collaboration and comradeship. It is a call that asks nothing short of remaking the world. It can be heard in a beautiful rejoinder to the Latin expression *omnia sunt communia* ("all things are to be held in common") and to its Zapatista-inspired transmutation "everything for everyone": the slogan that in the fall of 2023 spread through the streets alongside demands for a ceasefire—"Everyone for Everyone." If we can understand this world for how it is against children, then perhaps we can confront the ways that it is against all of us. What might we make of this world, for everyone, instead?

1

Dreams Called Childhood

During the first year of the COVID-19 pandemic, I would frequently wake up in the middle of the night, rattled by nightmares that concerned some version of the thought that my kid's childhood would soon be over. Often this prompted me to get up and check on them, sound asleep in their room across the hall. Then I'd go to the kitchen to spend the rest of my insomniac hours writing, if only to chase away the panic. I didn't know what else to do with the thought. I was reckoning with an inevitability. Some of the time, I convinced myself that it was *almost* an ideal circumstance, at least for this particular child, to transition into adolescence. But mostly, I was overwhelmed by sadness. It wasn't something I could get rid of; like this passage from childhood into adolescence, it seemed the only thing to do was to move with it.

It was in that period of maternal sleeplessness that this child, Z, began to speak of a recurring dream, the only one I've ever known them to have (for whatever that's worth). The dreams were set near the cabin where we'd moved to live with my father a few months into the pandemic, not long before Z's ninth birthday. In these dreams, they described small ponds forming everywhere outside, which they would follow until the ponds turned into streams, rushing down the mountain. They'd watch the water, fascinated, but with a sense that they had to keep themself from flowing downstream. These dreams weren't nightmares, they assured me, but more like adventures, animated by curiosity and wonder. And yet, each time they'd wake up, reporting that this dream had returned to them— always a little bit different, with new characters, details, and plot twists—I couldn't help but speculate about what was being washed away, and what it was that might never come back.

Thinking back on the way this dream emerged in this time, I'm struck by the stories we each took from it. Z would look forward to the dream's reappearance, wondering how it might change. I would hear it, each time, as yet another reminder of loss. The dream was about time I could not get back with them, all the moments I wished I could have handled better, in this child's short life. I did not miss the sleep deprivation I experienced while parenting and nursing an infant, but here I was, an insomniac anyway, unsettled by this sense of longing for which there seems to be no cure. I wondered, too: Would I look back on this next transition with such sadness as well? Was I, yet again, caught up in a time that could never be, taking for granted the moments ahead? Now years later, I find myself feeling that Z's childhood, if it was ever more than an idea, did not wash away. It merely dissolved into another idea, adolescence. And sometimes, not only in memories and dreams but in certain feelings between us, I find that their childhood reappears, however fleetingly, as if to remind us of what has been, and what can still be.

For all of us, perhaps, childhood is merely a dream. Dreams are where "the child with all his impulses survives," as Sigmund Freud argued, and it is through the interpretation of dreams that we uncover "the very wish which has given rise to the dream, and whose fulfillment the dream proves to be, has itself originated in childhood."[1] Conversely, childhood lurks as a dream, looming with us in the not-quite, in a desire for a future expressed as a past. It is the story of an unreachable fancy, as queer theorist Kathryn Bond Stockton writes, with the child as "the specter of who we were when there was nothing yet behind us," a figure of "who we are not and, in fact, never were."[2]

Here I consider this dream of childhood as a political problem and a way into the possibility of solidarity with children. Childhood is what we share in common; yet it is also what sets us apart from each other, and, indeed, from ourselves. Childhood "is only shared retrospectively by those adults who made it out," as historian Jules Gill-Peterson reminds us, in a world where so many children face "population-level killing projects directed intentionally" against them—Black children, Indigenous children, disabled children, migrant children, trans children, and poor children, who exist as what she calls "un-children." The idea of "the child," she suggests, "wish[es] away the inconvenience that almost no children qualify for its embrace. Its arithmetic is the stuff of the 1 percent." Though "un-children" is perhaps an "ugly phrase," as Gill-Peterson concedes, I find her reframing tremendously helpful, for a number of reasons. Certainly, it points us toward the disjuncture between childhood and the actual lived experiences of most children in the world. But more remarkably, it gestures at the potential for forms of intergenerational solidarity that will have to be salvaged from this wreckage. Whether we survive being children or not, we might pursue childhood as a promise it can never deliver—that which casts most everyone as un-children, as those who "must be harmed to sustain something deemed important."[3] Un-children is an opening for all of us, including adults, to struggle against the social conditions of so-called childhood, and to make sense of this dream, this nightmare, as part of the machinery of capitalist life.

To take on childhood as a dream is also to reckon with it specifically as a narrative. Childhood operates as a series of stories that we are told, beginning in early life, and that we learn to tell ourselves and each other. My interest here is in narrative as a political weapon: as a disciplinary instrument of adult power; but also as a tool to help us survive and find ways to unthink power. At least that is my hope, in turning now to stories of childhood.

§

So often the story of childhood is told from the standpoint of having ended. Perhaps a place to begin, then, is with the idea of a beginning—when childhood was taken up as an object of history.

One such moment came in 1960, when French historian Philippe Ariès stirred much controversy in proposing that until the seventeenth century, "childhood" did not exist.[4] In *Centuries of Childhood*, what many regard as the first major attempt to write a history of childhood, Ariès contends that through the Middle Ages and into the beginning of modern times, "the movement of collective life carried along in a single torrent all ages and classes," with children mixing with adults at about the age of seven.[5] There was "no room for a private sector" and, likewise, no need for boundaries between adult and child, or for the concept of childhood at all. A demographer, Ariès premised his history on the high rate of child mortality in Europe. Although records of infant mortality from this time are highly unreliable, it's estimated with broad consensus that in the Middle Ages, about one in three infants died during their first year, most often in the first weeks of their life.[6] A defining moment in Ariès's history came in the sixteenth century, with the growing popularity of portraits of dead children. "It is in fact quite remarkable that at that period of demographic wastage that anyone should have felt a desire to record and keep the likeness of a child," he writes, locating in the portraits of dead children a culture of inevitable loss.[7]

Like any provocation, Ariès's is easily picked apart. It rests on hyperbole and universalizing claims. Historians have widely disputed *Centuries of Childhood*'s use of evidence, citing flaws in Ariès's perhaps-wishful methodology and sweeping gestures. As child historian Hugh Cunningham remarks, "Ideas about childhood in the past exist in plentitude.... [Any] view of the world incorporates a view of the nature of childhood."[8] All historians of childhood face a fundamental obstacle: the vast majority of the documents and artifacts we have of the history of children's lives are written and archived by adults. Which is to say, histories of childhood should not be mistaken for histories of children themselves. Childhood is an idea constructed, quite clearly, from the outside. To the extent that we can understand this idea, it is as the inverse of supposed adult experience.

What's distinct about *Centuries of Childhood* is not its ambition but its particular conceptualization of childhood as a set of beliefs and practices about child-rearing, firmly situated in the mid-twentieth century. The major breakthrough of the book, despite its Europeanist grand narrative, comes from its denaturalization of the *idea* of childhood as an aspect of capitalist development. There are two key factors in this invention of childhood, which I'd like to trace out from Ariès's historical account as the premises of a specifically white, bourgeois ideal. At the heart of this ideal is a fantasy that persists today, in various mutations, of childhood as a period of incubation, during which the child is imagined as "not ready for life."[9]

The first of these factors is a revived interest of philosophers and political thinkers across Europe in education, beginning in the sixteenth century. Writing in 1575, Michel de Montaigne conceived of the correct education of children as "the most difficult and important problem confronting human knowledge."[10] Through the seventeenth and eighteenth centuries, most of the prominent figures of the Enlightenment wrote philosophies of education that were in some way contingent on a theory of the mind at birth. In his *Essay Concerning Human Understanding*, published in 1689, John Locke famously claimed that the child is born as a tabula rasa:

Let us then suppose the mind to be, as we say, white paper, void of all characters, without any *ideas*; how comes it to be furnished? Whence comes it by that vast store which the busy and boundless fancy of man has painted on it with an almost endless variety? Whence has it all the materials of reason and knowledge?[11]

Today, this idea of the child as a blank slate, not yet formed by experience, remains incredibly prevalent, providing the foundation for some of the worst forms of pedagogy—that myth of teaching as "molding young minds"—as well as contemporary theories of parenting. It is also an idea weaponized in accusations of indoctrination and "grooming," which transpose the agency of children onto the influence of adults.

Another pernicious philosophy of education from this period conceives of the child's natural state as one of "evil manners." In *Leviathan*, written during the English Civil War (1642–51), Thomas Hobbes contended that children are without any "rule of good" except for "the correction they receive from their Parents, and Masters."[12] In 1803, Immanuel Kant elaborated this conception of childhood as a process of moral development requiring both discipline and adult authority in his treatise *On Education*: "To grant children their wishes is to spoil them; to thwart them purposely is an utterly wrong way of bringing them up," he argued, deeming children's wishes necessarily prevented, as they "have not yet learned to control themselves."[13] In each case, quite crucially, we see the child function as a surrogate to the slave—as the Other who must bend to "reason" through domination, a fantasy that continues to propagate through Western colonialization.

In this assortment of Enlightenment-era treatises on education, Jean-Jacques Rousseau's *Émile* most closely resembles what we might today recover as a child liberationist philosophy, and not only because it offers a powerful critique of educational institutions, "fit only to make men double-faced, seeming always to attribute everything to others, but never attributing anything save to themselves."[4] Banned in Paris and Geneva the year of its publication, 1762, the book stirred controversy for its indictment of religion as an aspect of children's education. Three decades later, it would be foundational to the new education system of the French Revolution. For Rousseau, the child was yet to be corrupted. His notorious opening of *The Social Contract*, "Man is born free and everywhere he is in chains," should be read alongside this rejoinder from *Émile*, written a year later: "Everything is good as it comes from the hands of the Author of Nature; but everything degenerates in the hands of men."[5] Childhood, that is, must be protected and preserved. Defined through the threat of adult corruption, this notion of the child's innocence would have a profound influence on Romanticism—a reversal of the adult–child relationship based in reason, pronounced by William Wordsworth in 1798: "Could I but teach the hundredth part / Of what from thee I learn."[6]

The other key factor in Ariès's story of the invention of childhood is the ascendance of what he designates as the "modern family." Like the quarantined vision of education developing alongside it, the private sphere of the family household devised of childhood as a space and time of separation from society at large.

We see this private, domestic imaginary of childhood in the phenomenon of conduct books, which took hold of England by the second half of the eighteenth century. In envisioning the conventions of domesticity and family life, conduct books made explicit "exactly how the new order of household with a new form of authority at its center," as literary scholar Nancy Armstrong suggests, "was produced through education."[17] Mary Wollstonecraft's first publication, *Thoughts on the Education of Daughters*, is a prime example of this genre, drawing deeply from Enlightenment theories of childhood, while confined by the conventions of what today we might call a proto-self-help book. In Wollstonecraft's words, since "every kind of domestic concern and family business is properly a woman's province, to enable her to discharge her duty she should study the different branches of it."[18]

Far more than a book about child-rearing, *Thoughts on the Education of Daughters* can be read as a philosophy of motherhood, necessarily grounded in the white bourgeois household. Wollstonecraft's conception of motherhood incorporated what was otherwise deemed servant's work. This included advocating for breastfeeding, a contentious position at the time. With inflections of Locke's tabula rasa, she argued that breastfeeding was a matter of "laying the foundation of a good constitution": children "ought to be suckled by their mothers," she claimed, warning that children "who are left to the care of ignorant nurses, have their stomachs overloaded with improper food, which turns acid, and renders them very uncomfortable." By this logic as well, she suggests that "children very early contract the manners of those about them," and that "it is easy to distinguish the child of a well-bred person, if it is not left entirely to the nurse's care."[19] Much like the Lockean pedagogical fantasy of a void to be filled, Wollstonecraft's lactational dogma is imprinted everywhere in contemporary discourses of infant care, as a moralized version of motherhood that excludes most workers.

The literary output of conduct books reflects a broader turn to conceptualizing motherhood, the mother–child relation, and childhood as aspects of an intensifying family ideal of bourgeois society. By the eighteenth century, Ariès observes the formation of this ideal in the prominence of family portraits, which— in contrast to the portraits of dead children in the sixteenth century—position the child at the foreground of the family. "Everything to do with children and family life has become a matter worthy of attention," he writes, "not only the child's future but his presence and his very existence are of concern."[20]

In "Origins of the Family, Private Property, and the State," Friedrich Engels begins his story of childhood much earlier than Ariès does, locating it in ancient Greece, with the legal invention of monogamy. According to Engels, the monogamous family came into being as an arrangement of undisputed paternity, with the purpose of paternity as a system of inheritance: "the first form of the family to be based, not on natural, but on economic conditions—on the victory of private property over primitive, natural communal property."[21] Along with the private family, what Engels calls the "cellular form of civilized society," the figure of the child, and the concept of childhood, take form through this development. Throughout Ariès's historical narrative, the emergence of private property is a mysterious force, lurking in these fantasies of childhood, whether as education or family. But if there is a history of childhood at all, it is a history of a property relation, of the idea that children can be owned. So long as there is private property, childhood must be defined and limited by it, and we are left to speculate on what else childhood could be.

In the history of private property, the figure of the child must be understood alongside the figure of the slave. In the seventeenth century, children made up a large part of the Atlantic slave trade. Birthrate was a key measurement of productivity for slave owners—of this prime commodity, Thomas Jefferson declared that "a woman who brings a child every two years [is] more profitable than the best man of the farm."[22] Leading up to the Civil War, in the US South an estimated two-fifths of all slaves were under the age of sixteen, and a third were under ten.[23] Enslaved children began work as early as possible, often by the age of six. What is "childhood," in this sense, if not a form of privilege—even if that privilege is to be owned on different terms? Of the possibility of childhood in the context of slavery, Hortense Spillers describes an "enforced state of breach"—a state of a not quite orphaning, through which the child "had yet to be defined."[24] It is to exist deprived of rights, reduced to laboring bodies, as what scholar and writer Tony Brown articulates as a state of statelessness, as "almost not existing," at the brink of what it means to be human.[25]

Today, approximately 160 million children are child laborers. Their labor can be traced everywhere: in coffee beans from Brazil, Colombia, Costa Rica, the Dominican Republic, El

Salvador, Guatemala, Guinea, Honduras, Kenya, Mexico, Nicaragua, Panama, Tanzania, and Uganda; in textiles, garments, and "fast fashion" from Bangladesh, Burma, Cambodia, Ethiopia, Ghana, India, Indonesia, Nepal, North Korea, Pakistan, the Philippines, Thailand, Turkey, and Vietnam; in the majority of cotton, rubber, bricks, and timber, as well as rice, soy beans, corn, and sugarcane; in most of the world's bananas, cashews, cocoa, coconuts, palm oil, poultry, salt, tobacco, and yerba mate; and so much more.[26] In China, under conditions of forced labor, children make the toys that are turned into magical gifts from Santa, and the Christmas decorations too; they also make the largest portion of the world's electronics, as well as everything from artificial flowers to fireworks to hair products, not to mention aluminum, coal, and silicon. And in the US, although illegal use of child labor in meatpacking plants, agriculture, and other industries has been well documented, little is done to put a meaningful end to it.[27] Every morning there are tens of thousands of children who go to work in the gold mines of Africa, Asia, and South America. These children are at risk of dying in tunnels and mineshafts from explosions and collapse, from breathing in dust and toxic gas, and from starvation and dehydration, among many other factors. They work in conditions of extreme heat and prolonged exposure to mercury. Nearly half of the world's child laborers engage in what is rather euphemistically termed "hazardous work." About twenty-two thousand children are killed at work worldwide each year.[28] All of these children live in extreme poverty, about a third of them do not attend school, and many live without access to basic care.

What exactly is the *adult* world for these child laborers? While these children and un-children of global capitalism are quite clearly being deprived of childhood, it is also *as children* that they are far more vulnerable to exploitation.

Even the most fortunate of children in this world are subjugated by the legal definition of childhood, which restricts their freedom and enforces their dependency on adults. And each year, the World Health Organization estimates that up to one billion children experience physical, sexual, or emotional violence or neglect.[29] Nearly three in four children regularly suffer physical punishment or psychological violence by parents and caregivers.[30] Seventy-seven percent of substantiated child abuse cases involve a parent in the US, where the leading cause of death for children is homicide, and where more than seven hundred children die each year due to abuse or maltreatment from one or more parents or caregivers.[31]

It is as an ideal that the private family hides these miseries from public view. For the lucky few, the private family may represent something like a last resort of care in an utterly heartless world. Family retains the desire for something like an outside, a space of retreat and love—a state of exemption from the ongoing horrors of capitalist life. But it is under this regime of the family that "parents raise children in the face of incessant fear and anxiety. Their every act is mediated through an awareness of society's judgment," as queer communist authors Juliana Gleeson and Danyal Kade Griffiths write, while "children are taught to feel desperation and to accommodate themselves to capitalism by parents and other care workers living under capitalist conditions."[32] Childhood is, for the most part, a matter of survival, defined by a scarcity of care. And in this way, it is no different from adulthood. Yet under the conditions of childhood, to which many are subjugated well into their adult years, one has few rights and very constricted terms of autonomy.

By this point, you may have noticed that I have not offered a definition of childhood as a bounded stage of human development—something most likely delimited by more or less arbitrary legal benchmarks of adult rights and personhood, as in the ages of fourteen, sixteen, eighteen, twenty-one, and twenty-five, which in the US correspond with the right to consent to sex, to drive, to vote, to buy tobacco and alcohol, and to have access to health care as a dependent. More recently, in an executive order targeting trans children in 2025, the Trump administration sought to redefine the child and children as "an individual or individuals under 19 years of age," as part of a ruthless attack on access to gender-affirming care.[33] The reality of these legal definitions is something I've sought to unsettle, rather than avoid. These remain the parameters in which childhood is politically constructed, and the means by which some children, and not others, get to have any semblance of a childhood at all.

§

In troubling the idea of childhood, there is perhaps no better place to go than children's literature. Children's literature is where stories of childhood are produced, ostensibly, for children; it is also, inexorably, a topography of adult power. Even in the best of children's literature, we cannot escape this predicament: that everywhere we look for children, we find a property relation. We are also confronted with what queer theorist Rebekah Sheldon describes as the temporal disjointedness of the child, as a figure that directs us "toward a future formally foreclosed by its very constitution," she writes, "because the future the child points to is the adult who stands where the child no longer is."[34] In *Inventing the Child*, a study of childhood and fiction, literary scholar Joseph Zornado traces this disjointedness throughout children's literature: where adults construct a story for themselves "not so much from what really happened to them as children as from what they wished would have happened."[35]

Poet, essayist, and children's book author June Jordan once offered the question: "What do we have in mind when we give children a book?" She asks this while reflecting on her own commitment to writing *for* children, and on her curiosity about what that commitment entails as a practice of writing.[36] During the process of writing this book, I've come back to Jordan's question many times, hoping to uncover in some way what it means to write not necessarily for children, but *with* children.

Much of children's literature can be understood as written not for children but *to* children, baring a pedagogical function precisely as an expression of adult domination. Throughout the Grimm Brothers' fairy tales, published in two volumes between 1812 and 1815, disciplinary fantasies run rampant. Among these stories, the most succinct articulation of this disciplinary imaginary can be found in the tale of "The Willful Child":

Once upon a time there was a child who was willful, and would not do as her mother wished. For this reason God had no pleasure in her, and let her become ill, and no doctor could do her any good, and in a short time she lay on her death-bed. When she had been lowered into her grave, and the earth was spread over her, all at once her arm came out again, and stretched upwards, and when they had put it in and spread fresh earth over it, it was all to no purpose, for the arm always came out again. Then the mother herself was obliged to go to the grave, and strike the arm with a rod, and when she had done that, it was drawn in, and then at last the child had rest beneath the ground.[37]

The willful child's silence strikes at the very notion of childhood's beginning—where childhood meets the end of infancy, rooted in the French *infans*, "not talking." Following his pronouncement that "there is no such thing as an infant," British psychoanalyst and pediatrician Donald Winnicott argued that childhood starts when the "infant ego eventually becomes free of the mother's ego-support," at which point the infant can achieve "mental detachment from the mother [and] differentiation into a separate personal self."[38] Yet in the story of the willful child, it is the child's silence that acts as a symptom of her independence from her mother.[39] As feminist scholar Sara Ahmed notes, "We do not need to know any other details than that the child does not do what her mother wishes," but at the same time, "we do not need to know what the mother wishes."[40]

For the child, she is willful because she is silent, while she is silent because she has been reduced to her willfulness—to an arm that reaches out from the grave, which must in turn be buried through force.

In her reading of the story, Ahmed extends Gayatri Spivak's famous question "Can the subaltern speak?"—and more specifically, "Can the subaltern (as woman) speak?"—to the figure of the child. [41] As Spivak argues, the subaltern woman "cannot be heard or read," existing without history. Between patriarchy and imperialism, "the figure of the woman disappears," she writes, "into a violent shuttling which is the displaced figuration of the 'third-world woman' caught between tradition and modernization."[42] In the story of the willful child, the mother is likewise "obliged"—in her case, to strike the child's arm with a rod—but her obligation is always at odds with her child's willful condition. That is to say, for mother and child alike, the story is a warning.

Variations on the willful child appear throughout children's literature, nearly always to instill adult authority. A prominent version of this trope can be found in the figure of the feral child—an iteration of the noble savage. In Mowgli, the wolf child of Rudyard Kipling's *The Jungle Book*, colonial rule is asserted not through the parent but through parental absence. This unfolds as a conflict over the Law of the Jungle: while the Law "forbids every beast to eat Man except when he is killing to show his children how to kill"—as the narration explains, since "man-killing means, sooner or later, the arrival of white men on elephants, with guns, and hundreds of brown men with gongs and rockets and torches"—the tiger Shere Khan wishes to kill

Mowgli.[43] For the sake of the Jungle, Mowgli is ordered to leave by the Wolf Council, and he becomes willful, protesting to the panther Bagheera, "I was born in the Jungle. I have obeyed the Law of the Jungle." Eventually, Mowgli agrees to leave, promising the wolves that he will someday return, bringing the hide of Shere Khan. When he fulfills this promise, the pack begs Mowgli to stay: "Lead us, O Man-cub, for we be sick of this lawlessness." Mowgli refuses, however, and instead, as the story ends, he "became a man and married. But that is a story for grownups."[44] The "story for grown-ups" of Mowgli's adulthood, in this sense, is that of not only his willingness to become civilized but of his ultimate exertion of power over the Jungle.

This white imperialist trope of the feral child was taken up two decades after *The Jungle Book* by Edgar Rice Burroughs in the *Tarzan* stories, originally a serialized comic following the youth and adulthood of a British child raised by Mangani apes after his parents are killed somewhere vaguely on the West African Coast. Frantz Fanon and Edward Said both interrogated the *Tarzan* stories as colonial indoctrination. This entire genre of comics, Fanon argued, was "written by white men for white children. And this is the crux of the matter."[45] In Burroughs's Anglophilic and racist fantasy, as Said noted, Tarzan is extremely acculturated—whereas in the movie versions of this character, played by Johnny Weissmuller in twelve films between 1932 and 1948, what we find instead is "a barely human creature, monosyllabic, primitive, simple."[46] For Fanon and Said alike, Tarzan operates primarily as a figure of misidentification for young readers and viewers. All children will see themselves in "the good guys," as Fanon insisted, with the "young black man [identifying] himself de facto with Tarzan versus the Blacks."[47] This misidentification generates self-hatred in Black children, creating the psychological conditions to be dominated by white supremacy and adult supremacy as contiguous forces.

These literary jungles, where feral, "willful" childhoods meet the seeming destiny of colonial rule, share much in common with the island in the sky dreamed up by J. M. Barrie as Neverland, where Peter Pan and his "Lost Boys" exist forever outside of adulthood. Like Mowgli and Tarzan, Peter and the Lost Boys are orphans, another prominent trope of nineteenth- and twentieth-century children's literature. The orphan's predicament is as much a matter of willfulness as of survival—inseparable, as in the works of Charles Dickens, from a dream of being somehow rescued by the idea of an adult world. But conversely, in the case of Barrie's mythology, Peter's survival is predicated on his access to adult power, key to his rivalry with Captain Hook, and an ideal of white purity. Rather than a story of being rescued (and therein disciplined) by adults and the call of adulthood, Peter's eternal childhood functions instead as a fantasy of his own colonial and patriarchal domination over Neverland.

In Barrie's novel *Peter and Wendy*, these fantasies of domination appear most clearly in Peter's competing relationships with Wendy, Tinker Bell, and Tiger Lily, reaching a point of crisis in what's described as the "Night of Nights." On an otherwise-ordinary day in the domestic imaginary that begins to take hold of Neverland, Wendy feeds the Lost Boys while Peter is out of the house. So overwhelmed by the boys' complaints, Wendy cries to herself, "I sometimes think that spinsters are to be envied." When he eventually returns, Peter tells Wendy that she is "so queer . . . and Tiger Lily is just the same. There is something she wants to be to me, but she says it is not my mother." Peter asks Wendy what it is, but she refuses—"it isn't for a lady to tell"—"perhaps Tinker Bell will tell me," he scoffs. Then, as the narrator indicates, Peter has a sudden idea: "Perhaps Tink wants to be my mother?"[48] Throughout their exchange, it becomes clear that Peter understands his eternal childhood as dependent upon Wendy's coerced motherhood. More and more, he appears as the villain. "I am only a little girl," Wendy tells Peter. "That doesn't matter," he responds, "what we need is just a nice motherly person." In contrast to Peter and the Lost Boys, Wendy, Tinker Bell, and Tiger Lily exist somewhere outside the possibilities of childhood. Tinker Bell, trapped in fairydom, is envious of the way Wendy is seen by Peter, while Wendy longs to be seen as a "little girl." Tiger Lily lives in her own refusal of becoming married off and "staves off the altar with a hatchet."[49] For each, non-childhood is a state not only of exclusion but of captivity.

It is noteworthy that the character of Peter Pan initially took shape outside of children's literature, in a series of novels and plays written for adult readers. Before Barrie published *Peter and Wendy* in 1911, marking his first attempt to write about this mythology explicitly for children, he introduced the Peter Pan character in his 1902 novel *The Little White Bird*, followed by the play *Peter Pan; or, The Boy Who Wouldn't Grow Up* (1904), then the novel *Peter Pan in Kensington Gardens* (1906), and the short play *When Wendy Grew Up* (1908). Yet, as feminist scholar Jacqueline Rose contends, *Peter and Wendy* "has never, in any easy way, been a book for children at all," and "the question this throws back to us is whether there can be any such thing."[30] In its myth of the eternal child, *Peter and Wendy* exemplifies "the idea that childhood is something separate which can be scrutinized and assessed . . . the other side of the illusion which makes of childhood something which we have simply ceased to be"—and this is the fundamental problem of children's literature.[51] In other words, the wish for childhood to never end should be understood through this logic of childhood: as that which can only begin *as* ending.

We can trace these contradictions, and the suspicions they evoke, everywhere in the narration of *Peter and Wendy*. The narrator—clearly an adult, as Rose insists—is endowed with "the hindsight of one who is no longer a child, who can qualify 'children' with the 'all' of a total wisdom" and who "thus places at the safe distance of the third person the group which he goes on to describe."[32] For Rose, this peculiar voice subsumes the text as "a monument to the impossibility of its own claims." The narrator explains: "They"—as in *children*—"soon know that they will grow up, and the way Wendy knew was this. One day when she was two years old she was playing in a garden, and she plucked another flower and ran with it to her mother." The narrator continues, "I supposed she must have looked rather delightful, for Mrs. Darling put her hand to her heart and cried, 'Oh, why can't you remain like this for ever!'" The paragraph ends, "Henceforth Wendy knew that she must grow up. You always know that after you are two. Two is the beginning of the end."

The elsewhere of Neverland is the ideal of childhood we find ourselves simultaneously lost in and banished from, extending far beyond the narrative spaces of children's literature: a site of longing for what is forever out of reach, both parts a dream and a nightmare. Neverland summons what is desired of childhood through the dream of an island—that which, whether in joy or in fear, as Gilles Deleuze suggests, "dreams of pulling away, of being already separate, far from any continent, of being lost and alone," while it is likewise "dreaming of starting from scratch, recreating, beginning anew." The dream of an island is based in an ideal for which "there is something that precedes the beginning itself, that takes it up to deepen it and delay it in the passage of time."[53] This dreamscape of the island, like that of the jungle, illuminates in children's literature a sense of utopian longing about childhood as a not-quite-place, situated in an irretrievable past-yet-future, while at the same time rooted in an anti-utopian logic of adulthood. Inasmuch as expressing a shared desire for ongoing possibility, these spaces are defined in relation to a sense of foreboding impossibility.

With this, I want to return to June Jordan's question: "What do we have in mind when we give children a book?" As a writer of "allegedly children's books," Jordan ponders her own motivations: "I want to say to children, tell me what you think and what you see and what you dream so that I may hope to honor you." For Jordan, this is a practice of offering respect—a hope to convey to young readers, "I believe you can handle it, that there is a way and a means to creatively handle whatever may be the pain or the social predicament of your young life, and that I believe that you can and will discover or else invent that way, those means."³⁴ Instead of offering the fiction of a solution—a moral of the story that can be imposed on children, in some better form of adult authority—this offering of respect directs us to ways of moving into a shared predicament, and toward solidarity.

Liberatory representations of childhood may be few and far between. And we would be better off doing away with the notion that narratives have that purpose. However, when we give children a book, we can share something more useful than a representation of their liberation—handed down to them, like everything else. Among parents and caretakers, it's hard to avoid debates about what kinds of narratives children should and shouldn't be "exposed to," as some put it. Yet these debates often ignore the question of how to discuss and interpret these narratives together; they are not interested in helping children become active readers and critical thinkers, but are instead mostly resigned to raising children as passive consumers. Sharing a practice of reading with children is also a practice of listening to children: *What are you thinking about? What are your questions?* It's a practice of reading, together, against narratives of domination, of children and others. In learning to do this together as readers, perhaps we might also learn to do this with what lies beyond the page.

§

What do we desire from childhood—what can be saved from these dreams, shaped so much by the impossibilities of what we call adulthood? Thinking back on those nights of Z's recurring dream, early in the pandemic, perhaps I was anxiously awaiting something as I found myself unable to sleep: adolescence—a time so many experience as misery. Now my sleepless nights are spent wondering: What else could adolescence be?

Adolescence wreaks havoc on the child/adult dyad: it is where ideas of childhood and adulthood come into collision, revealing the instability of each. In this sense, parenting a teenager is often discussed in horrific if not tragic terms, as the struggle to reign over the rebel without a cause. By calling parental control and adult authority into question, however, the idea of adolescence also directs us toward ways to both imagine and enact solidarity. But in order to locate these potentialities, we must upturn the history of adolescence, particularly its role as a fantasy structure.

In 1904, the same year that Barrie's *The Boy Who Wouldn't Grow Up* was first staged as a theatrical production, American psychologist G. Stanley Hall gained wide attention for his characterization of adolescence as a state of "storm and stress," taken up in both biological and social terms in the decade to follow. While it was not until the late nineteenth century that adolescents appeared as a socially significant group, the term "adolescent" dates back to the fifteenth century in English and can be traced throughout medical discourse from the seventeenth and eighteenth centuries. During the nineteenth century, US and British newspapers often used "adolescent" as a metaphor for the nation in bloom.[55] But between 1869 and 1870, the term transformed into something more pejorative, with the appearance of phrases like the "temptations of adolescence," "feeble-minded adolescence," and "rabid adolescence" in publications such as

the *London Times*.⁵⁶ The year 1870, as Michel Foucault famously declared, also marked the "birth of homosexuality." With the
publication of German psychiatrist Carl Westphal's *Archiv für
Neurologie* on "contrary sexual sensations," homosexuality was
"transposed from the practice of sodomy onto a kind of interi-
or androgyny, a hermaphrodism of the soul," Foucault suggests.
"The sodomite had been a temporary aberration; the homosexual
was now a species."⁵⁷ In *A Queer History of Adolescence*, scholar
Gabrielle Owen tracks the adolescent's emergence within this
context as "simultaneously a site of discovery and disavowal"—a
figure of disruption, confusion, and transformation.⁵⁸

To the dream of childhood, adolescence is more often envisioned as a nightmare. We can trace this from the late nineteenth
century, when these figures of the adolescent and the homosexual began to take form in the literary imaginary of queer adolescence, most notably in Oscar Wilde's 1890 novella *The Picture
of Dorian Gray*. Much like Barrie's earlier Peter Pan narratives,
The Picture of Dorian Gray is a story of eternal youth, written
for adults. Like Peter, Dorian becomes trapped in a childhood
of sorts. Aging in his place is a portrait of Dorian, painted by
his friend Basil Hallward. As he looks upon the portrait, Dorian
despairs, "I shall grow old, and horrible, and dreadful. But this
picture will remain always young," and out of jealousy, he sells
his soul—"If it were I who was to be always young, and the picture that was to grow old! For that—for that—I would give everything!" Ultimately, Dorian's "beauty had been to him but a
mask, his youth but a mockery," of which the narrator describes
adolescence as a state of horror: "a green and unripe time, a time

of shallow moods, of sickly thoughts."[39] Yet at the same time, what Wilde conjures in this story is an antithetical vision of adolescence, as stasis and non-transformation—something more like the fantasy of adulthood.

Vladimir Nabokov's *Lolita* similarly unleashes the nightmarish from Barrie's mythology, in which we encounter something like Wendy's alter ego in Dolores Haze, the adolescent object of narrator Humbert Humbert's sexual obsession. While framed as a confession, note the manner in which Humbert attempts to reason with his reader, making use of different legal definitions of the child to justify his preoccupation: "Let me remind my reader that in England, with the passage of the Children and Young Person Act in 1933, 'the term "girl-child" is defined as "a girl who is over eight but under fourteen years" (after that, from fourteen to seventeen, the statutory definition is "young person").'" To this, Humbert expounds on the subcategory of the "nymphet," a variation on the queer adolescent. "I would have the reader see 'nine' and 'fourteen' as the boundaries—the mirror beaches and rosy rocks—of an enchanted island haunted by those nymphets of mine and surrounded by a vast, misty sea," he explains. "Between those age limits, are all girl-children nymphets? Of course not. Otherwise, we who are in the know, we lone voyagers, we nympholepts, would have long gone insane."[60] Who determines which "girl-children" are among these nymphets? Surely not them. Humbert's fantasy of the nymphet reveals something inherent about the figure of the teenage girl, whose identity is determined from the outside, based entirely on how she is perceived by a dominant adult figure.

Lolita was published in 1955, two years after Disney's animated feature *Peter Pan*—and however differently, both respond to the teenage girl as a new iteration of the adolescent, whose arrival was announced a decade earlier, by *LIFE* magazine's December 1944 issue: "Untouched by the war," the teenage girl lives in a world consisting entirely of "sweaters and skirts and bobby sox and loafers, of hair worn long, of eye-glass rims painted red with nail polish . . . of slumber parties and the Hit Parade, of peanut butter and popcorn and the endless collecting of menus and match covers and little stuffed animals."[61] She is, in other words, an ideal consumer, conjured by the advertising industry.

In inventing this figure, advertisers drew largely from the mid-twentieth-century fascination with adolescence among psychoanalysts. In 1950, Erik Erikson characterized adolescence as a conflict of identity and role confusion, among eight stages of psychosocial development he delineates in *Childhood and Society*: "[Faced] with this physiological revolution within them, and with tangible adult tasks ahead of them," he writes, adolescents become "primarily concerned with what they feel they are . . . [they] have to refight many of the battles of earlier years," while being "ever ready to install lasting idols and ideals as guardians of a final identity."[62] Similarly, Anna Freud theorized adolescence as a tumultuous process of returning to early childhood, while moving toward an adulthood which ultimately achieves a "state of normality."[63]

This notion of the teenager's unfinished (or not-yet-normalized) identity remains a powerful marketing tool—as the French-Italian radical collective Tiqqun once described of "the Young-Girl" in commodity culture, it is a figure that lives "in the illusion that liberty is found at the end of total submission to market 'Advertising.' But at the end of servitude there is nothing but old age and death."[64] Rather than achieving adulthood, the young girl becomes "a body entirely colonized by commodity symbolism," epitomized by anorexia, as "the fantasy of reducing oneself to physical purity: the skeleton."[65] In this sense, she "aspires to a perfection that would consist in having *no body*," as a figure of total annihilation.

Everywhere we turn, the adolescent appears monstrous—typified today as the monstering of trans youth. This monstrousness exposes a truth about childhood as well. Like monstrousness, as scholar Sara Austin writes, childhood and adolescence are "states of becoming . . . floating, frustrating identity categories."[66] The adolescent makes this monster state real, not just fantasy—that slowly, not suddenly, children change. Children are always changing. Children are no different from any of us in that regard. But change is always a threat.

The changeling is a version of this adolescent monstrousness, at the heart of so many depictions of puberty, for which menstruation and ejaculation impose particular horror. In Irish folklore, fairies steal children and replace them with their own, changelings who can never be fully human—just as the adolescent exists as not quite child, not quite adult. Through the figure of the changeling, the monstrous adolescent reveals that "what we really want is not so much an innocent child as an ignorant one, or at least we want to control the knowledge children gain and the way that knowledge is framed," as author Karen J. Renner suggests. The ultimate threat of the adolescent is that they will eventually "become so wise they can question our choices and values or notice our flaws."⁶⁷ In so doing, the adolescent rattles what we dare not question.

What if we reclaimed from these various pathologized, commodified, and monstered definitions of adolescence a set of contrary desires: ways of living against the disciplinary horizon of adulthood, the inevitability which so many narratives of childhood are set against? What if we were to reencounter the idea of adolescence as a process not of individual loss but of shared transformation? To do this means exhuming adolescence from its Latin origin, *adolescere*: "to grow to maturity." It means interrogating the latter notion—the point of arrival confused for adulthood—and placing the emphasis on the verb, "to grow." As opposed to childhood, forever in the past or the future, *adolescere* invokes an active present, enacted through collective practices, and the promise of ongoing change. It could lead us, perhaps, toward a political project of growing old, together—helping each other continue to live, open to possibility.

Growing old together is what we are doing anyway, whether we want to be or not. There is never a stage we can reach that offers us this stasis—supposed maturity—when we are not moving closer to death. Yet it is the denial of this reality that lies beneath these fictions of childhood, adulthood, and much else. It is the denial of this reality that keeps us from finding better ways to live.

They will not belong to the patriarchy.

They will not belong to us either.

They will belong only to themselves.

—Mary Peña and Barbara Carey, *Off Our Backs*

2

On the Possibility of Mothering

"Unless we recognize what we are asking mothers to perform in the world—and for the world—we will continue to tear both the world and mothers to pieces," as Jacqueline Rose warns us: it's when the world "cannot bear to confront its own cruelty that the punishing of mothers darkens and intensifies." And what we are doing to mothers has a name: *motherhood*. Like childhood, motherhood is an ideal. Yet as an ideal, motherhood is also, Rose suggests, the ultimate scapegoat—a mode of explanation "for everything that is wrong with the world, which it becomes the task—unrealizable, of course—of mothers to repair." Maternal failing is not only inescapable; it is also ongoing. If it is a matter of fixing the world on one's own, and being made to feel account-able for a world that cannot be transformed on such terms, then failure will always be there, hanging over everything. The idea of mothers, for the most part, stands in the way of our imagining ways of caring for each other in more collective terms.

But here, as your narrator, and as a person with the legal and social status of "mother," I must catch myself. Because in defining motherhood as this unrealizable task, I can't help but look for some kind of absolution. How tempting it is to punish motherhood for all the ways that it punishes us.

We need a different language for this problem. "The radical potential of the word mother comes after the 'm,'" as Black feminist Alexis Pauline Gumbs proposes: "It is the space that 'other' takes in our mouths when we say it. We are something else."[2] This possibility exists in the space between mother*hood* and mother*ing*. "Motherhood" is a noun: declarative, prescriptive. And "mothering" is a gerund, both a noun and a verb—or, as I prefer, a verb breaking out of a noun. "Mother," by extension, is also split. As a noun, "mother" is what one is called and, in worse cases, what one is made to feel obligated as. As a verb, "to mother" can be much else. "What would it mean for us to take the word 'mother,'" Gumbs asks, "more as a possible action, a technology of transformation that those people who do the most mothering labor are teaching us right now?"[3] This question courses through this chapter. It begins with the words we have for this idea of "mother" as what one is rendered, forced into, through attempts to care, but also as the longing for care, and the expression of that for which we do not yet have words. Where there is the desire called "childhood," there is also the desire to be "mothered"—and to the extent that we can all, somehow, understand the experience of being a child, we can also collectively imagine or strive to find new ways of mothering each other.

To be mothered goes both ways: one can be mothered, as in cared for; and one can be mothered, as in summoned into the labor of mothering. My mother mothered me in both senses of the word. First, as a child she mothered me *as a mother*—just as I, conversely, made her into "mother." Then, ten years later, she mothered me *as an older sister*. As my three half siblings were born during my adolescence, I gradually, perhaps irreversibly, learned to care for them in this peculiar way, without the expectation of being cared for myself. Years later I discovered a term for this in pop psychology: "eldest daughter syndrome." In hindsight, finding humor in this role has helped me make sense of it. But at the time, I discovered that I was seen as "mother" by the world as well. As a teenager carrying a child on my hip through public spaces, I was often mistaken for my siblings' mother. And this misrecognition sometimes felt like a threat. Sometimes it was indistinguishable from a violence that crept everywhere anyway. When I was thirteen or fourteen, I recall an older man at the grocery store winking at me and asking, "What aisle are they giving the babies out?" A few years later, the father of a child at my siblings' daycare center asked me out on a date, having made the assumption that I was a "very young mother"—or so he claimed.

Being maternalized, rendered "mother," can happen incidentally, unwittingly, if not coercively: those moments when one cries out, mutters, or perhaps just has the urge to declare, "I am not your mother!" As a teacher, it's hard not to notice how frequently some of my colleagues (and not others) face the implicit expectation of performing various forms of motherly care. In friendships, this maternal creep can be far more painful. Unlike the student–teacher relationship, friendship often holds an illusion, at least, of something like mutualism. The same goes for romantic relationships—as in the not-uncommon complaint "I want a partner, not a child." How easily one can be cast into this role of nonreciprocal care. Eventually one can feel that there was little to do besides fight their way out of it. In so many social and political milieus, this is a shared experience. And it is an expectation that ultimately can't be dodged: whether it is met, avoided, or outright rejected, there will always be consequences.

What does it mean to care for others when that care is coerced? And what does it mean to receive such care? What, if anything, sets that coercion apart from other nonconsensual dynamics? Or, more bluntly, I want to ask: How is that different from sexual violence? The difference is subtle: it comes from the fact that we are not attuned in the same ways to the violence of coerced care. We have to learn to look for it, for the slippages between these registers of violence.

But to be mothered—whether through receiving care, being made into a source of care, or finding the possibility of mutual care, however inconceivably—could be something quite revolutionary. For this to happen, as Adrienne Rich declared, "the institution of motherhood must be destroyed." As institutions devised by the private family and structured by its white, patriarchal fantasy, motherhood and childhood share a problem that pits mothers and children against each other. Thinking with Rich's proposition of *mothering against motherhood*, perhaps we can draw out terms of collective survival in what she describes as an imperative for "the mother's battle for her child—with sickness, with poverty, with war, with all the forces of exploitation and callousness that cheapen human life—[to] become a common human battle."[4] To interject, through the words of Audre Lorde, this is not and cannot be "only about those children we may have mothered"—it must be about "all our children together, for they are our joint responsibility and our joint hope."[5] Whether as children or as mothers, or as comrades in solidarity, we owe this possibility of mothering to ourselves, and to each other.

In order to make such a possibility even intelligible, if not actionable, what will it take to transform motherhood—or, as Rich insists, to destroy it? To this, Gumbs puts forth a different question: "What if mothering is about the *how* of it?" If we are to hold onto the possibility of mothering, it will need to start from the question of the *how* of mothering, in solidarity with children.

§

The *who* of mothering is another side of this question. What, for instance, could the *how* of mothering be for Margaret Garner? Garner was twenty-two years old and pregnant when she and her four children escaped the Maplewood plantation where they were enslaved in Richwood, Kentucky. They fled with Garner's husband, Robert, and eleven others on the night of January 28, 1856. Together they crossed the frozen Ohio River by foot, then split into groups, with the Garners heading for Cincinnati, where Margaret's uncle lived in a cabin outside of town. But soon after they reached the cabin, they were surrounded by US marshals, slave catchers, and Archibald Gaines, the owner of Maplewood. As they resisted, Robert managed to shoot two of the deputies. Yet they knew what would happen—they didn't stand a chance of survival. It was in that moment that Margaret reached for a butcher knife on the kitchen table and slit the throat of her daughter, Mary, who was two years old. But before she could kill her other three children, and herself, they were captured.

"What kind of mother/ing is it if one must always be prepared with knowledge of the possibility of the violent and quotidian death of one's child?" asks Black feminist scholar Christina Sharpe. "Is it mothering if one knows that one's child might be killed at any time in the hold, in the wake by the state no matter who wields the gun?"[6] The problem of motherhood, as an institution of property defined by white patriarchal power, is so clearly illuminated in the case of the enslaved Black woman, and the conditions of social death—which historian Orlando Patterson calls a *severed* natality. For enslaved women, the right to motherhood was never an option. As Angela Davis reminds us, "in the eyes of slaveholders, slave women were not mothers at all, their infant children could be sold away from them like calves from cows."[7]

Garner's three youngest children, including Mary, were each likely conceived through sexual violence at the hands of Gaines. Garner's story, however notorious, is that of the ordinary impossibility of enslaved motherhood—a mothering to be recovered outside the terms of maternal rights. In this contradictory sense, Garner's decision to kill her children was an act not only of maternal resistance but also of maternal care. In "[refusing] to forfeit her role as protector/mother," as cultural anthropologist Delores M. Walter writes, Garner killed her child in order to save her.[8]

At the time of her trial, Garner was derided in the newspapers as a "crazed and frenzied negress" whose actions were "brutal and unnatural."[9] Of her own words, however, there is little documentation. As some historians have asked, who speaks for Margaret Garner? In the absence of historical record, perhaps this requires the techniques of fiction. Toni Morrison famously took up this question in her 1987 novel *Beloved* through the character of Sethe, an escaped slave, who lives in a house she believes to be haunted by Beloved, the daughter she killed eighteen years earlier. Like Garner, Sethe has three other children. Her two boys left the house, while her daughter, Denver, has stayed. Though Sethe and Garner were born in the same year, 1836, the novel is set in 1873, years after Garner died of typhoid fever. In its endeavor to narrate not only Garner's impossible motherhood but her impossible future, *Beloved* is resolutely speculative; more than speaking for Garner, or even speaking with her, the novel speaks *toward* her, wrestling with the unbearable.

The closest that the narrative of *Beloved* gets to articulating this impossible motherhood comes when Sethe thinks back on what she could not say in the moment of her decision to kill her child: "I didn't have time to explain before because it had to be done quick," she remembers, "Quick. She had to be safe and I put her where she would be." Convinced that Beloved has returned to her as a young woman who appears at the house,

Sethe tells herself that she'll explain to Beloved "how if I hadn't killed her she would have died and that is something I could not bear to happen to her . . . she'll understand, because she understands everything already."[10] Sethe's motherhood is constrained by this logic, "if I hadn't killed her she would have died": it is a fugitive motherhood, a version of motherhood realized through a radical practice of what Hortense Spillers calls "actually claiming the monstrosity."[11]

As an inquiry into this fugitive motherhood, the greatest feat of *Beloved* comes from its shifting narrative perspectives, constructing a dialogue of the unspeakable as the basis of mother–daughter solidarity. Between the first-person narrations of Sethe, Denver, and Beloved, the novel unfolds through the double movement of being *mothered*—being made into mother while excluded from motherhood, on the one hand, and being cared for and made into the object of mothering, on the other. "I love my mother but I know she killed one of her own daughters, and tender as she is with me, I'm scared of her because of it," as Denver explains: "I don't know what it is, I don't know who it is, but maybe there is something else terrible enough to make her do it again. I need to know what that thing might be, but I don't want to." For Denver, to be mothered is to exist in this void of needing to know what she can't know. While she has grown up in isolation, in a house she also believes to be haunted, she witnesses her mother sink further into pain. In her adulthood, Denver realizes that her mother is trapped, "trying to persuade Beloved, the one and only person she felt she had to convince, that what she had done was right because it came from true love."[12] And in learning to mother herself, Denver learns to refuse the conditions of her mother's motherhood. A pivotal moment comes when Denver decides for herself that she is the one who has "to step off the edge of the world," and she reaches out to the community in town. But while Denver is supported by other women—former slaves, who understand her mother more than she ever could—she also discovers "a new thought, having a self to look out for and preserve."[13]

Revisiting Denver's revelation, I catch echoes of Audre Lorde's account of mothering. Just after her daughter had left for college, in 1983, Lorde describes what it means to "let her go into a jungle of ghosts" within a history of Black women who have given their children forth "into a hatred that seared our own young days with bewilderment, hoping we have taught them something they can use to fashion their own new and less costly pathways to survival." This is a collective knowing, she explains, of not having "slit their throats at birth tear out the tiny beating heart with my own despairing teeth the way some sister did in the slaveships chained to corpses and therefore was I committed to this very moment." In this collective knowing, Lorde finds the conditions of collective mothering: as she insists, "we can learn to mother ourselves."[14] For Denver, this is a recognition that suddenly animates her, following her encounter with Lord Nelson as she walks to town to find work. "All he did was smile and say, 'Take care of yourself, Denver,'" as Morrison writes, "but she heard it as though it were what language was made for."[15]

To care for and be cared for: What if language were made for this? To find what Gumbs describes as the "radical potential" of mothering involves digging further into the language. "Radical," meaning *rooted*, is also a process of uprooting—radicalizing. As the women from town eventually decide must be done for Sethe and her home, this uprooting takes the form of an exorcism. When thirty women assemble in Sethe's yard and begin to sing, their voices "searched for the right combination, the key, the code, the sound that broke the back of words." Their song built "voice upon voice until they found it" when it formed "a wave of sound wide enough to sound deep water and knock the pods off chestnut trees. It broke over Sethe and she trembled like the baptized in its wash."[6] This mothering against motherhood—breaking through, washing away, exorcising—is a necessarily collective act. And surely a part of collective mothering is a shared attempt to listen for Margaret Garner. It is a listening against motherhood, for a mothering that could have been, and with the hope that it can be still.

§

To get at the *how* of mothering is a relentless undertaking. And while there may be no promise of relief from the question, that isn't quite the point. It's more a matter of unbolting the verb from the noun of "mother," and of breaking open the spaces between the institution of "motherhood" and the ongoing activity of "mothering." Yet what always stands in the way of the revolutionary possibilities of mothering is the labor of mothering.

"They say it is love. We say it is unwaged work."[7] Once I encountered this declaration, at the beginning of Silvia Federici's

1974 Marxist-feminist pamphlet *Wages Against Housework*, I could not unhear it. But I have also grown to hear this with different punctuation. Rather than as a statement, it now appears to me as more of a question. And the question is about what can be discerned of love—romantic, maternal, and otherwise—if it cannot be untethered from unwaged work. Or perhaps the question is whether love and unwaged work—or any kind of work—are necessarily held in conflict, as if either (or anything) could be knowable outside the terms of the other.

The critique of the "labor of love" was integral to the rise of the International Wages for Housework movement in the 1970s, which framed housework, in Federici's words, as "the most pervasive manipulation, the most subtle and mystified violence that capitalism has ever perpetrated against any section of the working class," comprising everything from cooking and cleaning to child-rearing, romantic love, and sexuality. Capitalism hides this work as a natural, feminine attribute— but it is an imposed (if unspoken) social contract. "Capital had to convince us," Federici insists, to enforce the unwaged condition of housework, to believe that housework is not work, "thus preventing women from struggling against it, except in the privatized kitchen-bedroom quarrel that all society agrees to ridicule, thereby further reducing the protagonist of a struggle." In this reductive narrative, women are seen "as nagging bitches, not workers in struggle."[8] Much of Federici's argument revolves around the working conditions of this conflict between husband and wife, but, more importantly, it stretches far beyond mothers: housework, she contends, represents the common predicament of *all* women, for the ways that this work (like gender) appears somehow natural.

While I've learned so much from this critique of housework, I've learned more, perhaps, from troubling it. Most of all, I've grown suspicious of how the relationship of husband/wife, so fundamental to Federici's argument, effectively stands in for the relationship of mother/child as well. This gapes from a presentation she wrote for the second International Wages for Housework conference in January 1975, in which she declared that for women, "Sex is work." Federici asserts that as a result of sexual liberation, gendered labor has only intensified: while women were once "just expected" to raise children, she suggests, "now we are expected to have a waged job, still clean the house and have children and, at the end of a double workday, be ready to hop in bed and be sexually enticing." How does this logic—by which "for women the right to have sex is the duty to have sex and to enjoy it"—apply to mothering? While Federici leaves this question largely unanswered, it is the major barrier to overcome in this political project, if we are to recover forms of solidarity with children from its critique of domestic labor. The greatest potential comes from her assertion that in calling attention to what is work, "eventually we might rediscover what is love."[19]

Originating in the early 1970s, what would become known as the domestic labor debate was pulled into Marxological polemics over value production and became largely unconcerned with what we might call "the child question." At the very beginning of the debate, however, a child liberationist critique took form, marked for many by the 1972 publication of "Women and the

Subversion of the Community" by Mariarosa Dalla Costa. "The separation of children from adults is essential to an understanding of the full significance of the separation of men from women," she writes, posing an incisive analysis of the school system to which I'll return in the next chapter. Rather than conflating the housewife/mother's relationships to her husband and children, the essay seeks to uncover lines of solidarity between children and women, clarifying their shared miseries. When both children and women "are recognized as integral to history," Dalla Costa argues, "no doubt other examples will come to light of very young people's participation (and of women's) in revolutionary struggles."[20] In the social movements of the late 1960s and early 1970s booming in Italy, she observes something altogether new among youth—what she understands as "the autonomy of their participation *in spite of and because of* their exclusion from direct production." Women and children have been excluded, as she suggests, such that "the revolt of the one against exploitation through exclusion is an index of the revolt of the other."[21]

If we can't know each other, ourselves, and the possibility of what we call "love" between us, outside of our conditions of labor, then of course that goes both ways in the mother/child relationship. Selma James, who collaborated with Dalla Costa and later published an extended version of their argument, describes the first job of the woman (as housewife/mother) as "[reproducing] other people's labor power."[22] She does this for her husband, but also for her children. The housewife/mother is thus the unwaged worker, responsible for all that goes into caring for the waged worker such that he may carry out his labor, and the unwaged

manager, who must raise her children as future workers. Ultimately, the employers of the husband and the future employers
of the children are who benefit most from this, while—as Federici emphasizes most unequivocally—the housewife/mother is left
to personally endure the class conflict in relation to her husband
and children. The child, by extension, cannot know the mother
apart from these conditions.

What might the case for Wages for Housework look like
with children in the foreground, rather than the housewife/
mother? Children do not exist at the margins of this political
project; rather, they are its absent center. And while I find moments of child liberationist thinking, especially from Dalla
Costa, I wonder whether this framework relies, however uneas-
ily, on staging an antagonism between mothers and children.
As opposed to helping us to find solidarity, this critique of work
may instead pit us against each other even further, hardening
these roles of care*giver* and care *receiver.*

Years into the domestic labor debate, Angela Davis rather
decisively pointed to the ways Black women are excluded from
the political critique of Wages for Housework in the United
States, where the campaign had gained considerable momen-
tum in the mid-1970s. "Cleaning women, domestic workers,
maids—these are the women who know better than anyone
else" what is at stake in this campaign's central demand for wages, Davis writes: "In the United States, women of colour (and especially Black women) have been receiving wages for housework
for untold decades." In general, the domestic responsibilities of
women, which, in Federici's words, capitalism has naturalized as

"femininity," "provide flagrant evidence of the power of sexism," Davis agrees, but "because of the added intrusion of racism, vast numbers of Black women have had to do their own housekeeping and other women's home chores as well." As a result, "the demands of the job in a white woman's home have forced the domestic worker to neglect her own home and even her own children," she explains. "As paid housekeepers, they have been called upon to be surrogate wives and mothers in millions of white homes."[23] The paid housekeeper's state of enforced neglect of her own children marks the boundary between the work of mothering and the institution of motherhood—between a force of exploitation, and a system of hierarchy and exclusion.

It's hard not to stumble into the problem of mothers as a matter of surrender of some sort. The unfreedom of mothering cannot be told apart from the freedom of what it might mean to be able *to really mother*. To really mother: as in, to mother boundlessly, to both un-know and re-know mothering apart from motherhood. From every side of it, mothering is compromised. But in what ways—and for whom? I have grown to understand, in studying this as a feminist, worker, writer, thinker, and friend, and perhaps especially as a person who is called or made to feel as a "mother" in this world, that there is a revolutionary practice of mothering that must be purged from motherhood. It is not a matter of whether, but how.

Writing of her experiences as a participant in the early stages of the women's liberation movement, bell hooks recounts the ways many white, bourgeois, college-educated women perceived the status of motherhood as a political barrier and a "trap confining women to the home, keeping them tied to cleaning, cooking, and child care." Had Black women spoken up about motherhood, "it would not have been named as a serious obstacle to our freedom as women," she explains. "Racism, lack of jobs, lack of skills or education, and a number of other issues would have been at the top of the list—but not motherhood."[24] By contrast, hooks conceives of motherhood, sustaining "the very gestures of humanity [that] white supremacist ideology claimed Black people were incapable of expressing," as a *humanizing labor*.[25]

Rather than attempt to differentiate between competing "motherhoods" and conceptions of mothering, I want to sit with this notion of humanizing labor. Only in the context of labor as a social totality can *some* labor perhaps appear as humanizing—or, as I would prefer, something like *dis-alienating*. As a humanizing labor, in this sense, mothering is a practice of undoing what it means to labor, which takes place specifically through laboring. This is not a "labor of love." It is not labor disguised as something else, unwaged yet implicitly compensatory, naturalizing and therein enforcing work that is isolative but also actively de-collectivizing. It is a laboring that, if only in brief glimpses, and however indirectly, gets at the possibilities of what could be otherwise.

And we know this thing—and we know that we know it—but without being able to name it. It is felt in the difference between moments, the way that some can be so confining, and the way that others can open out so spectacularly. Perhaps the naming of it is beside the point.

§

We should reencounter these questions through a different problem (or perhaps a different version of the same problem): how to discern between the institution of motherhood, and the labor of gestation and birthing. On the one hand, this is the distinction that slaveholders monopolized, categorically rendering enslaved women as "breeders," shut out from the possibility of maternal rights. On the other hand, this distinction is potentially revolutionary, for the ways that it directs us toward our shared desire to care for each other, whether or not we describe this as mothering. If there are to be mothers in this world, may their mothering be a matter of choice and not coercion—and may we all be mothers, whoever may want to be. So much of the history of mothering, however, has been confused for what it never had to be: the logical, *naturalized* extension of gestation.

Another way toward this problem is posed as a demand. Author Sophie Lewis calls this demand "Full Surrogacy Now": the abolition of motherhood as a property relation. This abolition unties ideologies of maternality from the labor of gestation and moves toward a horizon of what she names the "care commune." Lewis explores the possibilities of this demand through a series of invitations. She asks that we envision "fully collaborative gestation" as a way of "manufacturing one another noncompetitively," and that we "hold one another hospitably, explode notions of hereditary parentage, and multiply real, loving solidarities."[26] In "surrogacy," she locates the revolutionary potential of *de-authorizing* the work of gestation, and de-linking that work from ideologies of motherhood. Turning to the global labor market of gestation, while looking for the conditions of possibility of collective care, she postulates: "If babies were universally thought of as anybody and everybody's responsibility, 'belonging' to nobody, surrogacy would generate no profits." She stretches this further: "Would it even be 'surrogacy' at this point? Wouldn't the question then simply be: how can babymaking best be distributed and made to realize collective needs and desires?"[27]

Solidarity with children will always be at odds with what we have learned to need from those called "mothers," and likewise, what mothers have learned to need from those who the world calls "their" children. The driving force of Lewis's demand is a transformational break from a logic creeping in most every notion of motherhood as the fantasy of the creator figure, whose life making is mistaken for proprietorship. In positioning the mother as life maker and therefore life owner, this fantasy also naturalizes the labor of pregnancy (and by extension, mothering, as well as womanhood). The "humanist idealization of 'fetal motherhood' rests on the conviction that gestation is not work," as Lewis suggests, but rather "the very pinnacle of wholeness and self-realization." To this, she rightly states what at least *should* be obvious: "Sometimes people can't become mothers; sometimes mothers die; sometimes they don't love their babies; sometimes they abort them, abuse them, abandon them, divorce their co-parent, or even kill."[28] What she calls the "tragedy of worldly contingency" is so often ignored in gestationally bound conceptions of motherhood, unfurling catastrophic harm on all of us, and most certainly on children.

Adoption and surrogacy bring this conflation of gestation and mothering into crisis—in some cases, not others, finding cultural acceptance through proximity to the institution of white, bourgeois motherhood. In this sense, Celeste Ng's popular 2017 novel *Little Fires Everywhere* presents a complex terrain of conflict between seemingly irresolvable versions of motherhood. Set in Shaker Heights, Ohio, the novel revolves around four women who come to personify these competing motherhoods: Elena is a rich, white, married mother who grapples with the truth of her ambivalence about having the last of her four children; Mia is a poor, Black, single mother who carries secrets of her own about the paternity of her child (and much else); Linda is a rich, white, married woman who endured years of fertility struggles before adopting a child; and Bebe is an undocumented Chinese immigrant who's starving when she makes the desperate decision to leave her baby to be rescued outside a fire station. Eventually, we discover that Mia's is a fugitive motherhood of sorts: she was hired as a surrogate and went on the run before giving birth, concealing this from her daughter Pearl. We also learn that Bebe's child has been adopted by Linda. And when Mia, who works with Bebe at a Chinese restaurant, decides to help Bebe reclaim her baby and take Linda and her husband Mark to court, the novel unsettles what it means to be a "mother"—and asks of the ways that mothering is bound up in conceptions of maker, owner, and caregiver.

While each of the mother figures in *Little Fires Everywhere* reaches a point of internal conflict, Ng's narrative poses its messiest, most compelling predicament between Bebe and Linda's versions of motherhood:

[Linda and Mark McCullough] had shown themselves to be exceptionally devoted to raising a child. Records showed that they had tried to conceive children of their own for ten years, and had been waiting to adopt for another four. They had sought the advice of every medical expert in the greater Cleveland area—including the best fertility doctors at the Cleveland Clinic—and then engaged the most reputable adoption agency in the state. Did this not suggest that they would give the baby the most loving possible care, along with every opportunity?[29]

To this—and note the parenthetical framing—the narration then shifts:

(But the baby already had a mother. Whose blood flowed in her veins. Who had carried her in her womb for months, who had felt her kicking and flipping within, who had labored for twenty-one hours as she made her way up faceup and screaming into the bright light of the delivery room, who had burst into ecstatic tears at hearing her child's voice for the first time, who had— even before the nurses had wiped the baby clean, even before they had cut the cord—touched every part of her child, her tiny flaring nostrils and the faint shadows of her eyebrows and the womb-slicked soles of her feet, making certain she was wholly present, learning her by heart.)[30]

Ultimately, the novel strains to make sense of these tensions, which it might otherwise disoblige itself from sorting out. Its power, instead, comes from staging maternality as its point of inquiry. But despite asking what it means to be a mother—"Was it biology alone? Or was it love?"[31]—and so clearly enunciating the problem of motherhood, the novel seems fixated on the idealization of "fetal motherhood" all the same.

Quite to the contrary, Lewis's call for "Full Surrogacy Now" demands something like the abolition of motherhood: "We are the makers of one another. And we could learn collectively to act like it," she writes. "It is those truths that I wish to call *real* surrogacy, *full* surrogacy."[32] This entails not only a radical decoupling of gestation from binary gender, with its trans-erasive and essentializing conceptions of maternality, but a doing away with the mother figured solely as a construct of the private family. Part of Lewis's point, of course, is to challenge our political imagination. That a world of full surrogacy, which no longer needs motherhood, seems outlandish to us should be instructive, if not galvanizing. It's in this spirit, however, that I acknowledge my own struggles with this provocation—specifically, with the ways that "full surrogacy" gets us toward the possibility of the care commune, a utopian vision I share with Lewis, and which our political work holds in common. That gestation is labor and a labor apart from mothering is particularly clear, and beautifully stated; the demand to collectivize and de-privatize care and create alternatives to the family as a regime of private property, scarcity, and domination makes perfect sense to me; and even conceptualizing practices of co-*parenting*, which refute the mother as a singular figure and naturalized resource, presents hardly an obstacle in my political thinking.

It becomes prickly, for me, with gestation itself. I can't fathom an experience more interiorizing and isolative, nor a labor more dangerous and potentially traumatic, than gestation. Whereas all labor is alienation, no form of labor seems as truly alienating. Could it be that through gestation, we get at what it really means to labor, in its purest sense: of robbing us of ourselves, sucking the life from us vampirically for the sake of continuing what is beyond us, however beloved or doomed? Perhaps I can't help but feel pulled down this line of questioning—it is an experience that can't be undone; it is an experience that undid me. And I am tremendously distrustful of its abstraction.

I pause to look at a person, thirteen years old as I write this, to whom I can only clumsily, if not embarrassingly, describe my connection. This person is a creature who came forth from within me, and I will not forget that: it was labor to bring them into this world, and it was labor that can't be reimagined from a series of other, painful experiences—miscarriages, health crises, a medically necessary abortion, a sequence of events that drew me out of any fantasies I might have previously harbored about my "bodily autonomy." I find myself recalling some of the dreams I had, throughout pregnancy, of this person not surviving. Sometimes, I would not survive either. It was a fear I'd never felt before. I do not say this to naturalize it—much of it was entirely *unnatural*, and quite alien. And by no means do I say this to idealize it. It's simply how I understood what was different about this work than other kinds of labor, including mothering.

Here, rather than as a continuation of pregnancy, mothering seems quite counterposed to gestation. To gestate is to absorb and sequester, to *host* in parasitic terms, to appear singularly as what exists multiply; whereas to mother is to nurture through separation, to break apart, and to become, in some ways, obsolete. Or at least I imagine this as the ideal of mothering, as a kind of care to be extricated from possession—and, likewise, from the experience of being possessed.

Whether or not it begins at gestation, mothering is exhausting, if not punishing. It can be difficult not to seek from the enduring conditions of this work something like a sense of ownership. And for this very reason, mothers will often feel entitled to acts of cruelty. It is still the case, as bell hooks made clear decades ago, that "feminist theory has not yet offered both feminist critique and feminist intervention when the issue is adult female violence against children." For the most part, she argues, feminist thinkers have failed "to call attention to the reality that women are often the primary culprits in everyday violence against children simply because they are the primary parental caregivers."[33] To any feminist claim regarding child liberation, this reality must be reckoned with.

In our vastly anti-maternal cultural landscape, there are of course plenty of depictions of maternal sadism, from the myth of Medea to *Mommie Dearest* and beyond. It is difficult to interrogate maternal sadism on any other terms. This is what struck me most about Japanese filmmaker Hirokazu Kore-eda's *Shop-lifters* (2018), which considers the difference between what it means to be a mother, and what it means to mother. The film begins with Osamu, a day laborer, and Shota, a young boy, who've just been out stealing groceries, deciding to bring a young girl back to their household, when they realize she's been left out of her house hungry, and in the cold. The analogy of theft, between shoplifting and kidnapping, is there from the start. But the young girl, who calls herself Yuri, was clearly being abused by her mother, who is in turn being abused her husband. Yuri's scars and bruises are first discovered by Hatsue, Nobuyo, and Aki, the women in what appears to be a family household, who begin to mother Yuri themselves. While Yuri's biological parents do not report their daughter missing, eventually Yuri's disappearance gains media attention. When Shota is hospitalized while trying to protect Yuri from getting caught shoplifting in a grocery store, the state intervenes, and the household unit is dismantled. Osamu and Nobuyo are arrested, Shota is put into a foster home, and Yuri is returned to her former household, where she continues to endure beatings from her mother.

However bleakly it might conclude, *Shoplifters* is an astonishing exploration of family abolitionist questions. As the film gradually reveals, none of this household of shoplifters and workers is related by blood. And if they are related by law, it is first and foremost as criminals. Upon their arrest, Osamu and Nobuyo are also charged with the murder of Nobuyo's abusive husband, whom we discover Osamu helped kill in order to protect Nobuyo. With Yuri, Nobuyo forms a bond from the shared experience of domestic violence. "If someone hits you and tells you they are doing it because they love you, they are a liar," Nobuyo tells Yuri. Then she hugs her, explaining, "This is what someone does when they love you." This moment, among many others between this not-quite-mother and not-quite-daughter, should be held in contrast with a later scene in which Nobuyo is interrogated about their relationship in police custody. "Children need their mothers," the police officer tells her. "That's just what mothers imagine," Nobuyo replies. Then she asks the officer, "Giving birth automatically makes you a mother?" The officer, a woman about Nobuyo's age, answers decisively, "You can't become a mother unless you do." Here, we learn that Nobuyo cannot conceive—something the officer is not only aware of but proceeds to hold against her: "I understand it's tough for you that you can't give birth. Were you jealous? Is that why you kidnapped her?" Nobuyo begins to cry, wiping her tears, looking away from her interrogator. "What did the two children call you?" the police officer asks. "Mommy? Mother?" Nobuyo continues to cry. "I wonder," she remarks, "I wonder . . . I wonder."[34]

Throughout *Shoplifters*, this question of what the children call Nobuyo and Osamu becomes a way of asking the bigger question of how to make thinkable this care and comradeship outside the language and material conditions of "family." While Osamu desperately wants Shota to call him "father," Nobuyo expresses more ambivalence about what to be called. Whether or not we ascribe an idea of family onto this collectivity seems ultimately a matter of interpretation. The film dwells in its uncertainties. But it also elaborates a vision of something like the care commune, most strikingly with depictions of shared meals. Gathered together in their small home, this collectivity slurps up noodles, passing ingredients to each other, paying attention to what Yuri will eat as she's brought into their space of mutual care. Finding and stealing food, bringing it to the home, preparing it, and sharing it is shown as a collective practice—they are bound not by blood but by meals, and, more generally, by their survival. Perhaps there is no need to find a name for this relationship between Nobuyo and Yuri. Or perhaps it's simply comradeship.

I'll return to Nobuyo's question: "Giving birth automatically makes you a mother?" As opposed to the police officer's assertion—"You can't become a mother unless you do"—I want to insist that we can all be mothers. And it is because we can all be mothers that we can also abolish motherhood. Yet it's at the precipice of this thought that I find myself in despair. What it takes for this to become imaginable, even in the slightest ways, requires much more than a shared dream.

And it is possible to do this imagining without indulging in anti-maternalism. Rather than maternalism, or anti-maternalism, what I am trying to describe as revolutionary mothering demands a dialectic of *anti-anti-maternalism*—a mothering to be found insurgently. Whether or not we call this mothering should not matter, but there is so much to learn from those who mother.

I sometimes wonder: if only everyone could dedicate at least one night of their life to caring for a newborn baby, to learn what that means and how it feels, outside the terms of a lifelong commitment. This would be of tremendous support to caregivers, but it would also bring us closer to fathoming how to care for each other collectively—and in concrete terms, not just abstractions. Those nights of sleeplessness, of waking continually and shutting down one's desire and need to care for oneself—for rest and sleep, and to dream—are so much of the time spent in some version of hellish loneliness. For those fortunate enough, the labor is shared with one or a few others. How rare it is, even among my closest comrades who speak and write so eloquently—and prolifically—of forms of collective caretaking, that one does this work outside some notion of parenting. It's an uncomfortable truth.

A friend of mine, who had a baby about a year ago, recently revealed that they had no idea how excruciating it would be not to sleep. It was how I felt, too. As a lifelong insomniac, I had convinced myself during pregnancy that I'd be up for the task. And maybe I was, in the same way that nobody actually is. Like my friend, it took me a while to speak about my struggles. I remember that a few months into it, an acquaintance of my partner's—a man in his sixties, a parent of two adult children, both about my age—reminded me that sleep deprivation is a form of torture. "You know that baby is brainwashing you," he jokingly told me. It stung. It's hard to prepare yourself for this kind of exhaustion. As my friend confessed—something the world coerces mothers into feeling they must do—their challenges were exacerbated by the sense of responsibility they felt to breastfeed, as a work that stretched out their experience of the bodily isolation of gestation, just when they thought it was somehow over.

However equal a partnership between a lactator and a non-lactator, just as between a gestator and a non-gestator, there is a disbalance we are encouraged to naturalize as "maternal." By the end of the first week of a newborn's life, most lactators are instructed to produce milk "on demand," varying from every hour to three hours.[35] Newborns should not go more than four hours without feeding in the day or overnight, meaning that REM sleep is difficult (if not unattainable) for the first months of caring for a newborn, especially if one is to consistently breastfeed. And as most lactators will certainly hear, consistency is crucial. You're frequently warned of those babies who get "hooked on the bottle" and won't go back to the nipple. By the end of the first month, lactators are instructed to produce up to five ounces of milk a day in feedings, while feeding between seven and twelve times a day. When I think back on that time, there were nights when I'd need to wake myself up, beside an infant fast asleep, so that I could lean myself against a pumping station in the living room to stockpile milk for my hours away at work. Regardless of lactation, however, all caretakers of infants are likely to struggle with sleep deprivation, with almost 40 percent of mothers averaging less than six hours of sleep per night in the first year.[36] And there is more of a difference between self-identifying maternal and non-maternal caretakers than there is between mothers who do and do not lactate. No matter how infants are fed, in conditions where they are cared for by one to two individuals, caretakers will suffer from intense sleep deprivation, with severe risks and often dangerous consequences, and this disproportionately yet unnecessarily impacts those we call "mothers." Here is an opening, if only we can recognize it: that we all could be doing this work, and finding ways to do this together, beyond the couple form of the nuclear family and the essentializing and highly atomizing pressure to *produce* care, and as a part of taking shared responsibility for a new life in this world. This could be entirely possible. Yet all the same, it seems painfully out of reach.

Rather than a culture of solidarity, what caretakers of infants all too often encounter is a culture of initiation. It's not just that when you know, you know—it's that supposedly you *can't* know, *until* you know. There is a logic of trial by fire that makes one a "mother," specifically. Unlike gestation, there is nothing about this labor that needs to be performed in this way. There is no biological constraint; there is no container, as in the womb, that excludes collective participation. There is an ideological barrier, which can absolutely be overcome. So much is left for us not only to dream up but to make tangible through practice.

What I'm driving at may seem obscure. Getting into this question has meant pulling apart gestation from motherhood, with the hope of finding something else—something like the utopian imaginary of "full surrogacy," although on different terms. Here, I look to another family abolitionist thinker, M. E. O'Brien, for what we might do with the collective practices that have been historically conceived in relation to mothering: "Instead of destroying the family, we must abolish it by preserving what is crucial to it—human love, connection, care, community," she writes, "without binding these qualities to a particular form of the household within capitalism." Abolition, in this sense, means "radically transforming these qualities, freeing them from relationships of coercion, abuse, isolation, and property."[37] To the extent that we can make thinkable the possibility of full surrogacy, I want to insist that we can also inhabit this alternate thought experiment: *we can all be mothers.*[38]

I first arrived at this notion at some point in the fall of 2014, with my friend and feminist co-thinker Marija Cetinic. Both of us were new mothers and somewhat isolated in our leftist milieus, living on different sides of the continent. We came together after wondering, on our own, about what to do with what felt like an accusation—what some choose to describe as "postpartum depression." While certainly, we each identified with elements of this medical condition, we were also uneasy about the ways this diagnosis biologized (and pathologized) the social conditions of post-gestational caretaking. More than that, we felt curious about how this diagnosis does and does not correspond with conceptions of maternality, with which we were also grappling.

It began as a series of letters. We asked each other questions. We shared our disappointments and confusions, and, slowly, we built shared insights. Our epistolary practice gradually transformed into an aphoristic project—short theses that together reached this particular demand, in our words at the time, to radically challenge the "distinction between mothers and non-mothers." This transition from our correspondence to collaboration felt quite miraculous. It had become a frequent comfort to send and receive updates on each other's thinking. But then, when those letters turned into a shared document, our words began to intermingle. While I look back on this project from a place of disagreement about some of the language we deployed, often hastily—and in utter exhaustion—I'm moved by the process it archives. We were writing toward what we hoped that mothering could be.

I took from my collaboration with Marija a set of core questions about this practice, which I want to break down and repurpose from within. I have no hope of thinking outside of mothering—nor do I especially want to. But I wonder how to de-individuate what it means to mother, and how to learn from the verb of mothering, to denominalize from this monstrous thing that insists some of us, but never all of us, must bear an impossible responsibility in perpetual solitude. While full surrogacy and this notion that we can all be mothers may be two sides of the same coin, there is a reason I am framing it as the latter. I cannot help but draw from my own experiences of mothering, as I think about the language to be used here, since part of mothering, for me, has meant talking quite extensively with children, including the child I brought into this world, about the problem of the private family, including the institution of motherhood. My reason is very simple: that *we can all be mothers* doesn't sound scary. And to not sound scary is actually quite important when it comes to solidarity with children. After all, too many things that children are told have the purpose of scaring them into submission.

Like any story one tells a child, you try to go about it in many ways. You practice, you experiment with the phrasing and where to place the emphasis, and you move differently through the story the more you anticipate how it will be heard. Speaking to children about the limits of the family form has been illuminating for me as a thinker. I've found that children understand it more easily than adults. I say this not to romanticize children's plasticity—a fantasy which Jules Gill-Peterson rigorously critiques in *Histories of the Transgender Child*—but to suggest that children reveal society's own immutability. That we might seek from more than just our mothers this thing we call "mothering" can open up a world of possibility for children. It is not a difficult proposition but a magical thought that sparks more thinking and generates curiosity.

All of us should take issue with the institution of motherhood, which harms caretakers and those they care for alike. But I wonder what might be salvaged from "the radical disorientation of joy" that Jacqueline Rose recounts of her experience adopting her daughter.[39] Simone de Beauvoir, in her foundational work of feminist philosophy *The Second Sex,* writes of children as bringing "joy only to the woman who is capable of disinterestedly desiring the happiness of another, to one who without reversion to herself, seeks to go beyond her own experience."[40] As Beauvoir notes, "Such an obligation is not at all *natural*: nature could never dictate a moral choice; this implies an engagement."[41] In other words: mothering is something we learn to do, for better and for worse. Too often conceived as an act of ongoing moral sacrifice, this state of what Beauvoir calls "disinterested desire" for the happiness of someone else is perhaps something that *all of us* could strive for. We could look to mothering, however imperfect and destined to failure, as a way toward mutualism, reciprocity, and collective practices of caretaking outside the framework of family relations. We could preserve the *pleasure* of mothering, as Rose suggests, while also struggling against what is wretched about motherhood in the private family, as an organizing principle of capitalist life.

§

I'm interrupted by some thoughts about my chosen genre: the essay, *essai*, or something like a "little attempt." Mothering, as I can only hope to have partially recovered from the constraints of motherhood in these pages, might be imagined as the ultimate act of *trying*. Mothering is a trying that anticipates the certainty of its failing; but it must be, also, a refusal of impossibility that takes place moment by moment, always incompletely. Mothering is not the solution. To look to mothering as a totalizing answer is to reproduce the problem of motherhood. Mothering is merely one of many places to start.

Remember,
you can have what you ask for, ask for
everything.

  —Diane di Prima, "Revolutionary Letter No. 19"

3

The Trouble with School

What do we want from school? To ask this is not to presume that what is wanted from school has much to do with what school actually *is*. While "schools are supposed to be places for children," as author and educator Eve L. Ewing writes, the history of schooling in the United States has been one of systemic miseducation, intrinsic to the settler-colonial racial project that persists in full force.[1] Children today endure a seemingly endless barrage of standardized exams, flattening the content of human history into bubbles on a Scantron, while their teachers live in fear of being fired or attacked for discussing topics of race, gender, and sexuality—and whatever else might reflect "anti-American, subversive, harmful, and false ideologies," as stated in an executive order by the Trump administration "ending radical indoctrination in K-12 schooling."[2] Far from a protected space of learning and care, schools are the battlegrounds of the most urgent political fights of our time.

To ask what we want from school is to probe certain desires that go largely unmet, with the hope of learning how else we might live. What are the promises of school—however little those promises may be realized? One way into these questions is through utopian imaginaries of the school. The attempt to imagine the ideal school can reveal a great deal about the fantasies wrapped up in schooling; and to speculate about what school *could be* helps us to understand the function of school in the dystopias in which we find ourselves.

As the Catalan anarchist Francisco Ferrer argued, critiques of school can take two modes of intervention: "to transform the school by studying the child and proving scientifically that the actual scheme of instruction is defective, and must be modified"; or to take the direction he proposed, in founding new schools based in an ideal of rejecting "the conventions, the cruelty, the trickery, and the untruth which enter into the bases of modern society." Ferrer established the Escola Moderna (Modern School) in Barcelona in 1901, conceiving the school as the seed of a society to come, against capitalism, the state, and military power, with the purpose of "preparing children for their entry into the free solidarity of humanity." In the years to follow, Modern Schools spread across Europe, drawing on Ferrer's pedagogical philosophy. Yet, to reimagine school in such terms proved incredibly dangerous work. For his crime of "having founded a school and a library," as novelist Anatole France put it, Ferrer was ultimately sentenced to death by the Spanish government, charged for orchestrating an insurrection against the renewed colonial war against Morocco known as the Catalan Tragic Week in 1909. His final words, as he faced a firing squad at Montjuïc Castle, were "Long live the Modern School!"[3]

Ferrer's murder galvanized an international movement, fo-
cused on implementing schools and continuing the project of
reimagining education. American anarchist Voltairine de Cleyre wrote of Ferrer's martyrdom as the "first loud articulation of
what has been asked in thousands of school-rooms, millions of
homes, all over [the] world"—a criticism offered most directly by children: "Who has not heard a child say," she asks, "'But
what do I have to learn that for? . . . What good does it do?'"[4]
Taking inspiration from the Modern School, de Cleyre proposed her own utopian vision of the Ideal School as "a boarding
school built in the country, having a farm attached, and workshops where useful crafts might be learned, in daily connection
with intellectual training," where children could have "free
contact with nature" and become "real doers in the world."[5] Ferrer himself was deeply inspired by his years in France, learning of the Prévost orphanage, where anarchist pedagogue Paul
Robin oversaw an experimental school from 1880 to 1894, in
the northern village of Cempuis. The surrounding geography
of hills, uplands, and valleys were key to Robin's approach to
integral education, which included walks on Thursdays and
Sundays, as well as daylong excursions about once per month.[6]

Far beyond the anarchist tradition, utopian inquiry into
schooling often takes this form of the boarding school in the
country. Like the dream of islands found everywhere in children's literature, the fantasy of the boarding school is vital to
narratives of childhood in Western culture, as in the ubiquitous
"coming of age" story which so frequently takes this particular
setting. Whether romantically or cynically, it is a setting imbued

with the pastoralism of the *campus*, Latin for "field," both outward and isolated. To the extent that the boarding school seems to exist at some mythical remove from the realities of adult life, including the private family, it is also a controlled environment—it crystallizes the trouble with school as a space of domination, which nevertheless presents itself as freedom.

These utopian/dystopian dynamics are easily found in the most dominant example of the literary boarding school in recent decades, J. K. Rowling's Hogwarts. While idealized as a terrain of young people's autonomy and discovery, Hogwarts operates as a system of extreme authoritarianism, made unambiguous by the "sorting hat" that magically determines each incoming student's class position within its scheme of houses. It is a vision of schooling and coming of age not so much as a process of philosophical and personal becoming (*bildung*), but as pure assimilation. Rowling's brand of anti-trans white feminism clearly aligns with this narrative world populated by "pure-bloods" and "half-bloods." By contrast, Kazuo Ishiguro, in his 2005 novel *Never Let Me Go*, engages with this literary setting in explicitly dystopian terms as Hailsham, the boarding school around which its narrative centers. In an act of rebellion that leads to her termination from the school, teacher Miss Lucy decides to speak up about the truth of Hailsham, where students are bred for their vital organs. "Your lives are set out for you," she explains to her students. "That's what each of you was created to do."[7] In Hailsham's "humane" mission, Ishiguro uncovers from this literary trope a eugenicist fantasy, lurking everywhere (however consciously) in Hogwarts and integral to the real-life history of boarding schools.[8]

The brutal legacy of boarding schools in North America haunts most every corner of this cultural imaginary. In the boarding school film of my youth, *Dead Poets Society*, the students mockingly refer to their school Welton Academy as "Hellton," but they come together to "suck the marrow from life" by retreating in the woods outside campus to what they call "the Old Indian Cave." Like the students trespassing, the film seems to hardly comprehend the colonial metaphor it stumbles into.

Beginning in the sixteenth century, under the pretext of "Christianization," so-called residential schools were instrumental to the genocide and cultural erasure of Indigenous people. In the US, the residential school system became federally funded by the mid-nineteenth century, followed by the Compulsory Indian Education Act of 1887, and then an attendance law in 1891 that sanctioned federal officers to remove Indigenous children from their reservations and homes by force. It was not until 1975 that these laws were fully terminated in the US, leading to the closure or drastic reform of schools in the years to follow. The last residential school in Canada was shut down in 1998.

The claimed purpose of education in the Indian boarding schools was "killing the Indian, saving the man." "The Indian was thought capable of being reconstituted, reeducated, and made into a more fully advanced human," as Sisseton Wahpeton Oyate scholar Kim TallBear explains.[9] This entailed cultural indoctrination and consistent abuse, along with a regime of forced labor. Upon entering the schools, children were assigned European names; they were ordered to speak English and prevented from practicing any cultural rituals; and they were made to wear uniforms and to give up their clothes and other possessions from home. Part of the initiation process at the schools involved cutting the children's hair as well. Dakota woman Gertrude Simmons looks back on the horror of this experience, when she was brought to a school in Indiana at the age of eight: "I cried aloud, shaking my head all the while," she recalls, "until I felt the cold blades of the scissors against my neck."[10] After children were integrated with such cruelty into the boarding schools, their "teachers" routinely whipped and beat them as part of the disciplinary process. Writing of the experiences of one of his relatives at St. Joseph's Indian School in Chamberlain, South Dakota, journalist, historian, and citizen of the Lower Brule Sioux Tribe Nick Estes describes the schools as a "smorgasbord for pedophiles and rapists."[11] Some children living in residential schools managed to run away, only to struggle without resources. Many children died in the schools due to the spread of disease, as well as starvation and neglect.

We're still learning how many children were buried in the unmarked grave sites that remain of these schools. In the US, at least fifty-three burial sites were discovered following investigations in 2022. In 2024, another investigation identified sixty-five former schools with burial sites. While hundreds of bodies of children have been found, researchers expect to find thousands, even tens of thousands more.[12] In Canada, where there were more than 130 residential schools in total, it's estimated that up to thirty thousand children died in the school system. These are children who have been lost to history, all in the name of "school."

For the child, as Emma Goldman once argued, school is "what the prison is for the convict and the barracks for the soldier," where "everything is being used to break the will of the child, and then to pound, knead, shape it into a being utterly foreign to itself."[3] In its violent histories, the boarding school lays bare this purpose of schooling, seen most starkly as an instrument of genocide: isolated, separated, controlled. In its literary fantasies of coming of age, the boarding school is necessarily understood as a *false utopia*. Beneath its shallow promises, it functions as what Michel Foucault described as a "protected place of disciplinary monotony."[4]

It should come as no surprise, then, that the most liberatory cultural representations of boarding schools diverge from the utopian premise of "coming of age." Instead, many take their focus on what scholar Andrew Scahill calls the figure of the revolting child—the child who reflects "no need or desire to become [the] replica of their adult counterparts." If we are to imagine childhood as being set apart as "a transient state of not-yet-becoming," he writes, "then the horror of the revolting child is that he or she is locked in a liminal stasis predicated on contradiction"—that of being "already-arrived, both-at-once, growing—but not growing up—in a land of never-never."[5] The revolting child's very existence threatens the social order, as we find throughout the history of this trope in film. After its first screening in 1933, Jean Vigo's short film *Zéro de conduit*, which tells the story of a student uprising at a French boarding school, was banned for twelve years by the French government. Years later, Lindsay Anderson's film *If...*, very much an homage to *Zéro de conduit*, received the highly prohibitive X rating. Nothing menaces the adultist world more than the possibility of the child who does not wait until adulthood—to come of age, that is—for some semblance of freedom, precisely because that freedom is unknown to adults as well.

While these representations of revolting children indicate little interest in utopian imagination, their power comes from dismantling the false utopianism of schooling—and from putting us into contact with the question posed at the beginning of this chapter: What do we want from school?

The revolutionary stakes of this question might be understood as the political unconscious of *If....*, made and released in 1968, amid student uprisings across the world. Although these events remain in the background, they animate the film's sense of insurrectionary possibility. Upon its theatrical release, *If....* scandalized audiences with its conclusion, in which a small group of students open fire from the rooftop of their boarding school during a Founder's Day ceremony. Their uprising may seem naively dangerous, if not dangerously naive, yet through the course of the film we see the conditions of this revolt created by the school's power structure, upheld by students in the service of adult power. The "whips" are students placed at the top of the hierarchy, charged with disciplining others into submission, and enjoying certain exclusive privileges in the school. What's most threatening about this group of revolting students, who call themselves "the Crusaders," is their total lack of interest in becoming whips themselves. As Mick (Malcolm McDowell) professes to his comrades, "Violence and revolution are the only pure acts."[16] In shooting at the headmaster, teachers, parents, alumni, and fellow students, the Crusaders act as mere symptoms, and knowingly so. Their revolt, as Anderson later insisted, "is inevitable, not because of what they think, but because of what they are. . . . If [their] story can be said to be 'about' anything, it is about freedom."[17]

By far my favorite film about student revolt, *Bambule: Juvenile Reform—for Whom?*, faced even greater barriers of censorship than either *Zéro de conduit* or *If. . . .*, largely due to the controversies surrounding its screenwriter, journalist and Red Army Faction member Ulrike Meinhof.[18] Ten days before the film's planned release in Germany in 1970, Meinhof went underground with several other RAF members, after liberating the political prisoner Andreas Baader. Six years later, Meinhof was found dead by hanging in her prison cell, awaiting trial, while the film would remain unseen until much later, when it was televised in 1994. But even without the context of Meinhof and her political legacy, there is something palpably dangerous at work in her screenplay, which pressurizes the frustrations of its adolescent characters and their desires for revolution.

Bambule was inspired by student activists and residents of West Berlin *borstals*—state-enforced reform schools for youth from proletarian families who had dropped out of or been expelled by the traditional school system. Meinhof would let some of them stay at her apartment or raid her kitchen, and she listened to their stories about everyday life at "school"—more accurately, both parts prison and factory. The film takes place in the fictional borstal Reinickendorf, where adolescents sing of their incarceration together:

Reinickendorf, you killer of my youth!
Reinickendorf, you madhouse!
With more frequent leave we surely wouldn't abscond.
We often went over the walls.
Cops screamed, "Stop!" but those cunts didn't catch us.
Oh, beautiful freedom![19]

The student-prisoners of Reinickendorf seize what they can of this beautiful, if not unfathomable freedom, of which smoking cigarettes seems like the closest approximation. Taking its title from the German prison slang for "riot," *Bambule* steadily moves toward a climactic final scene, set in "the hole," where two of the central characters, Irene and Iv, have been confined. They discuss what it might mean to break out of the borstal. "We do an action, and what happens?" Iv asks from a place of defeat, "Cops come, and then nothing." Irene pushes back: "We will do it again! If you obey, they are happy because you are ruined. Then they are cool because they have crushed you." As she listens to Irene, Iv goes silent. Then, suddenly galvanized, she asks the closing line of the film: "Who is guarding tonight?"

That we never see the riot in the borstal is crucial to the film's political imagination. As Iv tells Irene, "When we don't know what we want, we can't do anything about it." Unlike the final moments of *If....*, *Bambule* ultimately refuses to indulge us with its impending insurrection. Rather than a violent spectacle, the film ends with a tender examination of the shared desires of young people who know what they want to escape but can hardly envision a life apart from it. What these films have in common is not some utopian vision of education but a set of revolutionary questions. As Mick asks his comrades, "When do we live? That's what I want to know."

Or perhaps we should ask instead: When do we live, if not during this time of schooling? The collective tragedy of school is this shared longing for childhood, what is always never-not-now. It strikes at what we hold out for, no matter our age: a place away from this one, where we are free to discover even more than ourselves.

§

Among the times in my life when I've witnessed political acts of solidarity with children, perhaps the earliest came in October 1992. It was about a month after my seventh birthday. I don't remember whether I saw it when it happened or merely heard about it afterward, but so many adults seemed to have something to say about Shuhada' Sadaqat (née Sinéad O'Connor) after she ripped up a photograph of Pope John Paul II during her performance on Saturday Night Live. What I remember was feeling confused. As with the disappearance of Pee-wee Herman from my life the year before, I had virtually no explanation, only suspicions. The talk all seemed to be moving around something, and never through it.

A decade later, I was no longer confused. When the *Boston Globe* published its historic investigation of child molestation by priests in the Catholic Church and its private school system, it felt as though the "facts" were catching up—a feeling that came rushing back in the fall of 2017, with what became the #MeToo movement. We'd known all along, in different ways, about Catholic schools, based on how we'd participated in this conspiracy, however consciously. Perhaps this shared knowingness was expressed as casual suspicion, in more of a joking manner—the kinds of jokes that, for a long time, would degrade that crazy woman Sinéad O'Connor, and whomever else. It was also carried as secrets, for ourselves and for each other. By then a teenager, I sensed this possibility of solidarity with children once again through the shockwaves of investigations into the church. As a child I had survived sexual abuse, and over the years that followed, I witnessed the man who abused me convert to Catholicism. While many around him seemed shocked by this strange turn for a once-outspoken atheist, I wasn't. It was perfectly clear what this conversion offered. I didn't grow up going to church, but I knew other children who were forced to go, and who shared their sense of fear without ever having to say it directly. There was hardly a point in verbalizing it. What would it amount to, in speaking up, if not more to be afraid of?

So much of this abuse continues to happen under the guise of religious education. This was the primary responsibility of former priest John J. Geoghan, one of the abusers identified in the *Boston Globe*'s initial exposé, who molested children consistently for three decades, during which he had been moved to six different parishes in the Boston area. When the investigation was published in January 2002, over 130 people had come forward with stories of being violated or raped by him. In providing "spiritual counsel," Geoghan preyed on low-income families, often with single mothers who were most vulnerable to shame and guilt of neglect. According to Joanne Mueller, a single mother with four boys who lived in Melrose, Massachusetts, Geoghan offered to take her kids out for ice cream and also help around the household, reading them stories and putting them to bed as Mueller cleaned up from dinner. Later she discovered he had been raping the children. In her deposition, she recalled one of her sons explaining, "We couldn't tell you because Father said it was a confessional."[20]

The church's private school system is integral to these horrors. A survivor of child sexual abuse, David Lorenz recounts the power an abusive priest had over the college prep school he attended in Northern Kentucky. As the school guidance counselor, Earl Bierman had a close relationship with almost every student in the school. It was not uncommon to go to Bierman's office. "During some of these counseling sessions that I had with him," Lorenz later testified, "he would often turn the topic to one of my personal sexual development and under the guise of this discussion would grope and touch me inappropriately." As Lorenz got older, Bierman's role as guidance counselor became even more blurred with something like friendship. Bierman would frequently invite Lorenz and his friends to his house, sometimes hosting "sleepovers." It was during one of those sleepovers that Bierman, as Lorenz recalls, "all-out assaulted and abused me and a friend of mine." In Lorenz's words, "I couldn't resist because I was raised to respect adults and teachers and do as I was told. This was especially true if the person was a priest—a holy man of God."[21]

As many survivors of abuse in the Catholic school system attest, they experienced confusion between religious pedagogy and "grooming," often following instructions framed in explicitly spiritual terms. Child abuse is a rampant issue across all schools. It is by no means specific to Catholic schools, but it is intensified by the isolation of children under this system. Abuse of power, whether in the form of sexual violence or otherwise, has been protected in the Catholic school system due to its unique political position outside the state and the private family household alike. In the US, the Catholic school system continues to be the largest entity of nonpublic Christian education. Most Catholic elementary schools are run and owned by local parishes, and most Catholic secondary schools are run by a diocese or archdiocese. The ostensible autonomy of this school system makes the children within it even more vulnerable. For the same reasons that evolution and slavery can be legally excluded from the curriculum of Catholic schools, the history of child abuse and the Catholic Church has been largely disregarded. As I write this, the majority of states in the US (thirty-three) do not require clergy to report information about child abuse to police or child welfare officials.[22]

Without moralizing state authority, or deferring to mandatory reporting, we should look to this exemption of clergy as indicative of the role of the state in this conspiracy of the Catholic Church. This organized abuse of children is not a problem that the state will resolve. Nor is the solution parental rights—rather, such logic only exacerbates the problem because it fundamentally understands parents to be the owners of their children, regardless of whether that involves caretaking at all.

"Parents don't want [some kids] to be aware . . . and that's the parents' right": this is what Anthony Merante, principal of St. Bernard Elementary School in Pittsburgh, explained to NPR in 2018, following a grand jury report about child sexual abuse in the city's diocese. The report named seventeen out of sixty-four elementary schools and high schools, detailing accounts of molestation and rape in the school, as well as grooming during the school day. On the first day of school that September, two students at St. Bernard led their classmates in prayer. Along with leaders of the world, and the sick and suffering, the students prayed for victims of abuse in the Catholic Church. Otherwise, the recent grand jury report was not mentioned during the service. It was but a brief moment of children acting in solidarity with each other in the face of adult power.[23]

Every day, children go to schools where they are bullied by other children or abused by adults. Children are sent by adults who are legally responsible for their safety and care, without being warned of or prepared for the potential dangers they may face. What children *do* learn of their endangerment often emerges from radical moments of solidarity. These are moments whispered from child to child, sometimes in the form of secrets from the adult world. Sharing secrets is how so many of us survive childhood, if we can. Because children listen to each other. This is one of the most common practices of collective care that children create together. If we are to learn about solidarity with children, it must begin with listening, and believing.

§

During the two years following the COVID-19 outbreak, I trained myself to teach online classes while parenting a child as they adapted to the conditions of "remote learning." In the routine we eventually developed for our days, Z and I spent the mornings alongside each other at our desks, and in the afternoons they played outside as I continued to work. Through my window, day by day, I watched them develop a game called "dog school." The game was very elaborate, involving a binder filled with lesson plans, exams, attendance records, and report cards for our dogs (and later our cat as well). Stella, a vigilant old cattle dog, found this activity of being schooled quite exasperating, though she did her best to follow the instructions of her teacher. Mona, a puppy at the time, was more of a challenging student. At times, the game struck me as tragic. Wasn't there a world beyond school to dream up in this time? Was there any room to imagine something else? Eventually I came to recognize that something more radical was transpiring. This is not to deny the tragedy but to appreciate that a desire was also being explored. Z was messing with the script of school, along with its premise of adult authority. And perhaps it requires making a mockery of school to salvage what the idea of school robs from all of us.

Thinking back on this time, it seemed that there was no choice but to be inventive about school. As a teacher, I felt overwhelmed by this task, though also privileged to stay employed while caretaking from home; as a parent, however, I was much more motivated to make the most of it, surely because of my collaborators in this experiment. Z became an avid reader, spending long afternoons stretched out on the couch with chapter books, or listening to mystery and science fiction novels on audiobook in the bathtub or the kitchen. They took up the alto saxophone, began to sew and make clothes, researched birds and then dinosaurs, and recorded lists of classic films to watch, many of which we did. My partner and I took them hiking and backpacking, and we learned to identify fungi, wildflowers, snakes, and lizards. These are among the experiences I cherish most of all in our life together.

But I don't mean to romanticize this period. Under orders to "shelter in place," children were exposed to an immeasurable surge in domestic violence. Many children experienced neglect for a variety of reasons, ranging from abuse to lack of resources. The knowledge of this, what the UN would later call the "shadow pandemic," was always hanging in the background. And even within the safety of our "pod" of children, parents, and caretakers, there was never an illusion of autonomy from the regime of schooling. For a few hours, almost every day, we worked on "real" school. There were worksheets, assignments, Zoom videoconferences—along with a pressure to *catch up*, intensifying with the anxieties of getting *left behind*.

Since then, these pressures and anxieties have taken form as a generational accusation of "learning loss." Research indicates that 31 percent of students in the US have "fallen behind" in math and 26 percent have "fallen behind" in reading.[24] Young people continually face pressure to make up for this supposedly lost time—a time when nothing seemed to have happened, with the denial that anything else could have been learned. The learning loss narrative has also been called an "achievement gap" in today's youth. Children, teachers, parents, and caretakers are bombarded with these narratives of crisis, everywhere from school districts and administrators to fearmongering journalists and political talking heads to family members, neighbors, and friends voicing their concerns. In a rather standard *New York Times* op-ed from the allegedly "post-pandemic" spring of 2023, Tom Kane and Sean Reardon, directors of educational policy research centers at Harvard and Stanford, argue that no amount of fearmongering will be enough to contend with this *deficit* of learning. "Most parents remain ill-informed about how far behind their children are," they suggest, offering a solution in the form of more work—"learning opportunities"—assigned to students over summer, after school, and on weekends. They take this further, making a case for a thirteenth year of school. "If we fail to replace what our children lost," they warn, "we— not the coronavirus—will be responsible for the most inequitable and longest-lasting legacy of the pandemic."[25]

The "we" in this formulation is worth sitting with. It is a generalized adult "we," but with specific targets—its purpose is to distribute blame. Whereas solidarity might be found between students, teachers, parents, and caretakers in a struggle against this injunction to "replace what our children lost," the narrative of this "we" sets all of us against each other, in a battle to catch up. But catch up to what exactly?

Childhood, as I've already discussed, is so often conceptualized in terms of loss. While children are told to enjoy their years of youth "because you'll never get them back," they're also told to work as hard as possible to *get ahead*, or to *catch up*.

Although all adults were at some point children themselves, it's preposterous that so many adults today pretend as if they understand what childhood has been like since the onset of the COVID-19 pandemic. I often encounter this adult chauvinism in my job teaching first- and second-year writing courses in a university. It's hard to avoid a palpable attitude about "kids these days" and their inadequacies coming from some direction. But the conditions of our education system were already in a state of perpetual crisis—the pandemic has simply made that reality undeniable. For the foreseeable future, the "learning loss" of the pandemic will be discussed in the way that carbon dioxide in the atmosphere *should* be discussed: as the marker of something concrete and measurable, which could improve our collective survival if we're able to reach a particular level. Students will be assigned more and more work, while being systematically deprived of the time and space for dreaming, discovery, and play. As a teacher, when I hear about the supposed deficiencies in today's youth, after all they've endured during the pandemic especially, it hardly aligns with what I've observed in this time as a parent and caretaker to other children. It never accounts for what Z has learned emotionally, inhabiting this world-historic health crisis and all its uncertainties, or for what they have learned politically, in witnessing global capitalism assert itself.

Part of what many children have learned in this time came from a different narrative, for which adult anxiety over "learning loss" was instrumental. It was a narrative many children knew was a lie: that returning to school as soon as possible was in their best interest. So many children knew that if their health and well-being were the actual issue at stake, they wouldn't be put back into classrooms before vaccines became available. They knew that their safety mattered less than the fantasy of going "back to normal," whether or not they understood the motives of economic recovery. They knew that this was not about catching up—that no matter what, they would continue taking more standardized tests, designed to reduce knowledge to a statistic, and that that had little to do with how or what they learn. Being lied to in this way has politicized many young people, and we're only beginning to see the impact of this.

When the classrooms reopened at Z's school, they did not want to go back. We listened. They expressed anxiety about getting sick, getting us sick, and getting their grandparent sick. They wanted to wait, and we were able to let them. But so many children felt the same way and didn't have that option. They were sent back to schools—what panicked caretakers were referring to as COVID "death camps" at the time—and their consent did not matter. What we did as parents did not comprise a solution. It was an act of desperation, in a situation of limited options, and in which we had more options than most.

I had never planned to "homeschool" as a parent. In fact I was deeply suspicious of homeschooling as a phenomenon. Some studies claim that homeschooled children are no more likely to experience abuse than students at public or private schools, but this is also impossible to substantiate because children are at far-greater risk for abuse going unreported or unnoticed in the context of homeschooling.[26] Today the case for homeschooling, in lockstep with the charter school movement that took off in the 1990s, reflects a deeply anti–public school agenda, primarily based in Christian-right values: parents who want the right to prevent their children from learning "critical race theory" and purportedly being "groomed" by trans-inclusive educators. During the paradigm of "remote learning," homeschooling became an appealing solution for reactionary parents, suddenly involved in their children's educations and outraged about the curriculum—leading to the accusation of teachers indoctrinating their children. By and large, homeschooling is a vision of education premised on the rights of parents, not of children. Though there has been significant political work to create systems of accountability for homeschooling households, such as the Coalition for Responsible Home Education, homeschooling cannot resolve the trouble with school, nor can it be an answer to the question of how to build solidarity with children. In the absence of any clear solutions, however, it can be a strategy.

The philosophy of homeschooling with which I most closely align is that of "unschooling." Black feminist and child liberationist Akilah Richards shares an encouraging account of unschooling in *Raising Free People*, a parenting book published as panic over "learning loss" began in 2020. She reflects on the summer break of 2012 as an experiment that became a "rescue mission," when she and her partner "took that chance [and] followed our daughters' requests for more time to do what they wanted." Unschooling was key to this political breakthrough: "This singular focus on the best way to educate our daughters billowed out into liberation work," she explains, describing it as "a practice of acknowledging and pivoting away from oppressive, control-centered relationships among people of any age over to something that centered consent, community, and lifelong learning."[27] Richards inspires us to think about what unschooling looks like on broader terms, while understanding that this model of education is limited to radical parenting. Her conception of raising free people generates vital questions about how to parent and caretake against the logic of parental rights, and how to extend unschooling beyond the confines of the private family.

The idea of unschooling was first developed by author and educator John Holt, whose 1974 manifesto of sorts, *Escape from Childhood*, opens with a list of rights that should be made available to any young person, and which largely do away with the legality of parenthood. These rights include: the right to be "responsible for one's life and acts," to "direct and manage one's own education," to "make and enter into, on a basis of mutual consent, quasi familial relationships outside one's immediate family," and to "seek and choose guardians other than one's own parents."[28] What's most useful about Holt's pedagogical philosophy of unschooling is how it dismantles the relationship between adult power and schooling. At the same time, as a practice, it is for the most part constrained to private households, including all variations of "collective living" that, however antagonistically, are similarly atomized. This is not what unschooling has to be.

For Holt, unschooling originated primarily as a case against compulsory schooling. He wrote of education as a system of oppressing children and their capacity as thinkers, calling it "perhaps the most authoritarian and dangerous of all social inventions of mankind."[29] And he came to this conclusion after years of working as a public school teacher, trying to improve the education system from within. Eventually, he decided to take his efforts outside the classroom and began developing a critique of schooling in his first book, *How Children Fail*, in 1964:

> To a very great degree, school is a place where children learn to be stupid. A dismal thought, but hard to escape. Infants are not stupid. Children of one, two, or even three throw the whole of themselves into everything they do. They embrace life, and devour it; it is why they learn so fast and are such good company. Listlessness, boredom, apathy—these all come later. Children come to school curious; within a few years most of that curiosity is dead, or at least silent.[30]

The best way for adults to help children to learn, Holt argues, is not "by deciding what we think they should learn and thinking of ingenious ways to teach it to them"—which characterizes so many well-intended approaches to pedagogy—but instead "by making the world, so far as we can, accessible to them."[31]

As a principle of caretaking and building solidarity with children, unschooling offers a vision that is expansionary rather than a mere model for homeschooling within the private family. Unschooling is a way of relating to schooling, no matter one's position within or outside any given school system. When Z eventually returned to school, once it felt safe for them, we were still unschooling. When they come home in the afternoon from the public school they now attend, we discuss what was taught in class that day. We talk about the political questions that come up—how to participate in a #CeasefireNow walkout, how to show up for a friend who's struggling to come out to their parents, how to process the "9/11 class" each fall, how to advocate for their pronouns to be respected by teachers and classmates, and much else. We read and learn together in dialogue with school, and regularly through conflict with the curriculum of the school system. In discussing these issues, we are unschooling in that we are questioning the world together, and insisting that there is life beyond schooling.

§

Unschooling, homeschooling, or various forms of social justice and radical pedagogy will never be enough to take on the trouble with school in its totality. As individual parents, caretakers, and teachers, we have to develop ways of collectivizing these practices. The struggle needs to extend outside of households and classrooms, and toward a broader project of liberation. This would involve a revolution of *deschooling*, what Austrian philosopher Ivan Illich elaborated as a social transformation based in the disestablishment of the school system.

In his 1971 treatise *Deschooling Society*, Illich envisioned the conditions for a liberation movement that starts in school, which "could foreshadow the revolutionary strategies of the future." This educational revolution would be guided by the following goals:

1) To liberate access to things by abolishing the control which persons and institutions now exercise over their educational values.

2) To liberate the sharing of skills by guaranteeing freedom to teach or exercise them on request.

3) To liberate the critical and creative resources of people by returning to individual persons the ability to call and hold meetings—an ability now increasingly monopolized by institutions which claim to speak for the people.

4) To liberate the individual from the obligation to shape his expectations to the services offered by any established profession—by providing him with the opportunity to draw on the experience of his peers and to entrust himself to the teacher, guide, adviser, or healer of his choice. Inevitably the deschooling of society will blur the distinctions between economics, education, and politics on which the stability of the present world order and the stability of nations now rest.[32]

As opposed to models based on isolationism, such as homeschooling, deschooling is directed toward a communization of education and critical thinking, which is necessarily intergenerational as well: it begins with the recognition that schooling isn't just for children.

"We are all involved in schooling," as Illich writes, "from both the side of production and that of consumption."[33]

Schooling is our social totality: it is everywhere, and it is inescapable. There are no individual solutions to this predicament; indeed, it is necessarily understood in terms of collective struggle. In this regard, Illich's initial conception of deschooling should be recovered from the free market solutions to the school system proposed in his 1973 follow-up, *After Deschooling, What?* This is a matter of discerning the process from the program in his work. Regarding revolutionary strategy, he provides an essential insight: "The risks of a revolt against school are unforeseeable," he acknowledges, "but they are not as horrible as those of a revolution starting in any other major institution, [since] school is not yet organized for self-protection as effectively as a nation-state, or even a large corporation."[34] With the increasing privatization of universities, however, this will continue to be less and less the case.

The Gaza Solidarity Encampment emerged as a powerful form of deschooling and solidarity as I began writing this book. Students were creating Gaza Solidarity Encampments in universities across the world, calling for an end to the Palestinian genocide, and demanding institutional and governmental divestment from Israel. Perhaps nowhere more than in schools are the political contradictions of this moment so clear, as we watch institutions of "critical thinking" systematically retaliate against students and teachers who actually engage in critical thought. At Columbia University, students who have taken courses such as "Genocide Studies" collectively decided to put their education into practice—but this is exactly the line at which schooling asserts its control. It is what distinguishes between matters of "free speech" and "campus safety." What's most dangerous about the campus is what can be called dangerous. And in this scheme, mass arrests and police violence against students and teachers do not count.

Today we are seeing the acceleration of what cultural critic Samuel Catlin calls "campus panic." It is not a new phenomenon: "From Vietnam to Gaza, it has never let up," as Catlin explains. "Reliably, every few months something happens 'on campus' that the media inflates to the status of a national emergency," which are circulated as "scandals so fascinating and disturbing that they eclipse even a genocide."[35] By resisting the fantasy of the campus, he suggests, we can also begin to resist this campus panic: "The Gaza Solidarity Encampment itself demonstrates this lesson. The students involved in the protest refused to be cast as the Child in a national fantasy. Camped out on the campus, they instead occupied that fantasy. Offered a panicked, irrationally terrified future of security for some, they courageously demanded a future of freedom for all."[36] By occupying the physical space of the campus, students are deschooling in the sense of taking back their education and re-creating it as collective power, while also demanding the transformation of school in concrete political terms. Both parts free school and blockade, the encampment reflects the revolutionary strategies essential to deschooling society.

As this movement of encampments grew in the spring of 2024, campus panic has grown with it. The fight against this panic is a struggle not only against the ideological fantasy space of campus, but against the hatred of students. "The anti-student imaginary is full of massacres that aren't happening, rather than the ones that are," scholar Daniel Spaulding quips. In his essay "On Hating Students," Spaulding elaborates on the revenge fantasy at the heart of campus panic: "Arrogant snowflakes meet the real world, where facts don't care about your feelings; would-be radicals get job offers rescinded; would-be gender theorists get their dignity stripped in low-paying service jobs." To this, he suggests that the student is defined by "susceptibility to discipline": "A student is a person to whom an expanded range of disciplinary procedures can be applied, since they are at the mercy of multiple sovereignties," he writes. "Thus, students can be simultaneously arrested by the NYPD, evicted from their homes, and suspended from academic programs. And in Gaza, they are being killed."[37]

Among academic workers, what has been politicizing for us as "nonstudents"—who are nevertheless targets of this revenge fantasy ourselves—has come from collectively witnessing this hatred of students as a structural condition of schooling, rather than as a mere exception playing out right now. We receive countless emails about threats to "campus safety" from the same campus administrators who oversee police violence against hundreds of students, resulting in arrests, hospitalizations, and inestimable harm. We are told that our job is to support our students, but to keep our jobs we are asked to betray them. However we position ourselves as individuals, we are acting within a system that disregards, and in some cases seems to outright hate, its students.

Throughout these recent struggles, some of the most politically galvanizing moments have come from students and teachers working together against the repression of university administrations. Never before have I witnessed such a show of student–teacher solidarity. Among the many who, like myself, have spent their lives as students and academic workers, perhaps something like a glimpse into a deschooling society emerged on April 22, 2024, when dozens of faculty linked arms and formed a line around protesting students, after their employer, New York University, ordered the NYPD to raid the Free Gaza Encampment in Gould Plaza, a block from Washington Square Park. Days later, faculty at the City University of New York created a picket around their campus encampment as well, chanting, "To get to our students, you'll have to get through us." And days after that, the first faculty solidarity encampment was formed blocks away at The New School, which called on "faculty across all campuses to escalate and take greater coordinated risk in solidarity with the student movement, their demands, and the people of Palestine and their righteous struggle."[38] "[Most of us] had taken part in the student encampment—offering teach-ins, helping with resources, and just hanging out," as my friend Natasha Lennard, who teaches at The New School, explained to me at the time: "We wanted to act in solidarity." Soon after the faculty encampment was established, students and faculty and other supporters moved to take over the entire university building together.

These moments of student–teacher solidarity help us to imagine education in revolutionary terms. And this involves confronting the trouble with school—not by opting out of it, as in the libertarian impulse of "unschooling," but by remaking school in order to remake the world.

In his vision of revolutionary education, Belgian author and former Situationist Raoul Vaneigem calls for students and teachers to come together to form collectives tasked with "snatching the school from the glaciation of profit and changing it to a place of simple human generosity." As in Illich's call to disestablish school, Vaneigem makes a compelling case to take back the schools as the basis for revolution: "Occupy your school; don't let them appropriate you for their programmed dilapidation," he writes. "Transform the schools into creative workshops, into meeting places, into parks of attractive intelligence."[39] While the encampments reflect this transformation, part of their power comes from a shared practice of critical negation. Inasmuch as the encampments illuminate aspects of a revolutionary pedagogy, they also expose the ways that educational institutions are not designed to educate, forcing their contradictions to the surface.

Inspired by the Free Gaza encampments, Trans Kids Deserve Better, a group of youth activists in the UK, began to experiment with these tactics during the summer of 2024. In August, they occupied the Department for Education in

London with a series of demands to improve trans youth's conditions of safety and learning in schools, while facing governmental bans on puberty blockers and access to gender-affirming care. "I'm out here because I want school to be safe," one of the youth activists explained. "I have never felt safe as a trans person in school."[40] And by taking autonomous action, they were showing adults how to show up for them, beyond the idea of "protecting trans kids": "The adult supporters who've been around have been supporting us how we need and that is, to me, a representation of how the wider movement around trans youth liberation should be," as one protestor put it. "Trans youth organizing themselves and calling the shots and taking these matters into our own hands."[41]

For youth and adults alike, what these occupations and encampments created were zones of contact with what school—and the world—could be, if only we try for it. And to try, we have to practice what schooling makes impossible: solidarity.

Is there further to go? Of course, because there is always more to come, there is always further to go. . . . There is a future which we imprisoned spirits cannot even glimpse.

—Louise Michel, *Red Virgin: Memoirs of Louise Michel*

4

Child Liberation

A Utopian Problem

It might be helpful, from here on at least, to read this book as something along the lines of science fiction. But this first requires some reflection on what constitutes science fiction—and parsing that from what so frequently science fiction is tasked with. Ursula K. Le Guin once lamented that the problem with science fiction has to do with the genre's perceived responsibility to *extrapolate*. Writing of this misperception in the author's note to her 1974 masterpiece *The Dispossessed*, Le Guin argues that extrapolation is "far too rationalist and simplistic to satisfy the imaginative mind, whether the writer's or the reader's." Science fiction, she maintains, "is not predictive; it is descriptive."[1] Indeed, while prophecy is not the purpose of science fiction, it is often the expectation, and as much the reason why some are drawn to science fiction as the reason why others seem to avoid it. As Le Guin suggests, we should instead pursue science fiction as a thought experiment. This begins as a practice: "Open your eyes . . . listen, listen."[2]

For Octavia Butler, similarly, science fiction's responsibility is not to predict the future but to "make use of our past and present behaviors as guides to the kind of world we seem to be creating."[3] In this sense she describes the genre as a kind of revolutionary parenting of the future: "Our tomorrow is the child of our today," she writes. "Through thought and deed, we exert a great deal of influence over this child, even though we can't control it absolutely. Best to think about it, though. Best to try to shape it into something good. Best to do that for any child."[4] To imagine the future, in other words, is not about making predictions but about examining the problem of the world together, as a form of collective care.

Child liberation is one such science fiction among many. It is something to approach delicately, without indulging the dream of a complete political program, but with the hope of piercing through the fissures of a social totality—the "adult world" of capitalism that is likewise against most adults—and nurturing the possibilities that ooze from it, however we can. It is a partial inquiry into the revolutionary conditions of the present. As a thought experiment, child liberation is a utopian problem: it confronts our own unfreedom to imagine.

All utopias are problems. What a burdened (and burdensome) idea, utopia; what miracles it is expected to perform. Utopia is doomed to failure so long as it is bound to the false concept of perfection. In turn, the utopian thinker may seem to be a fool who, for whatever reason, never internalized this common sense: that perfection is, of course, impossible. But to reduce utopia to this cursed pursuit would be to entirely ignore the problem (and indeed the joke) posed by Thomas More, who coined the term in the sixteenth century as a play between the Greek for "good place" (*eu-topos*) and "no place" (*ou-topos*). This isn't a surprise: it is by ignoring problems that we've all learned, to varying degrees, to survive; and it is also how we've learned to cope with what stands in the way of our collective survival.

Shutting down problems is the business of anti-utopianism. Precisely in its invitation to question and reckon with uncertainty, a utopian problem stirs up claims of certainty—that is, the certainty of what can and cannot be. "[The] case against utopia continues to revolve around a fairly stable set of indictments," as Marxist-feminist scholar Kathi Weeks explains. "Speculation about alternative futures is, from the perspective [of] classic anti-utopian ontology and epistemology, at best naïve and at worst dangerous."[5] Child liberation epitomizes this dual threat in utopian thought. Adult power represents the final vestige of unquestioned "natural" order in this world, hence its vital role in justifying and maintaining all other forms of domination, through the *infantilization* of the disempowered. Which is to say, adultism is the ultimate anti-utopianism.

Most reactions to child liberation are not so much a matter of utopian thought as of dystopian dread: *Lord of the Flies* comes to mind, or *Children of the Corn*. Children are imagined as a danger to themselves and to others. Whether for liberals or for the Christian right, children aren't trusted to be liberated— that would go against what it means to be a child: unthinking, subservient, dependent, messy, irresponsible. Before we can even wonder to ourselves what child liberation might mean, the line of inquiry is quickly thwarted. With each question of what freedom for children—and for all of us—might look like, we are met with statements about why such freedom could never be.

Take Sam Leith, author of *The Haunted Wood*, a history of children's literature, who dedicated an essay in the spring of 2024 to respond to a forthcoming book from philosopher Lorna Finlayson on the issue of child liberation. Leith had not read Finlayson's manuscript. All Leith seemed to need was the announcement of her book's acquisition for publication to rouse his condemnation. "Children are maniacs. Left in charge of their own lives, they will subsist entirely on Lotus Biscoff Spread eaten from the jar with a dessert spoon," he contends. "Were we to take seriously the notion that children should be put in charge of their own destinies, I feel confident we could reverse the goods of western civilisation, patiently accumulated over millennia, in a generation or two." To make his point, Leith then proceeds to humiliate his own children: "Children, in my experience as the parent of a 14-year-old, a 13-year-old and a 10-year-old, are not to be trusted with implements any sharper than a butter knife," he claims, adding that "the last time I gave my 12-year-old freedom of movement, he left his guitar lesson, climbed on the W3 bus instead of the 144 and my co-oppressor, his mum, [had to] go and rescue him." Not surprisingly, Leith sees his children and their "delinquency" as fair game (they are his private property, after all). It's tempting to meet Leith's speculation that perhaps Finlayson has never "even met any children" with some speculation about his "parenting style." But he makes no effort to hide his adult supremacy: "There's a whole two-century long, hard-fought history of campaigning to remove rights from children," he maintains, "and personally I'm all for it."[6]

Adult supremacy operates through an explicitly anti-utopian logic. The ideology of "no alternative" is all that matters; it has little correspondence with the legal limits of adulthood. "Children" today are often just people who are younger than you—or perhaps just people who are *lefter than you*. Even among themselves, adults are relentlessly pitted against each other as more and less "adult," as in more and less precarious. In this toxic culture, whether one is employed, insured, partnered, familied, and so on comes to measure one's adult status.

We talk around, but never quite through, the mundanity of capitalist crisis in generational conflicts. My generation "came of age," one might say, during the 2008 financial crisis, and since then we have been derided for the *immaturity* of our financial decisions (e.g., our penchant for lattes and avocado toast, which has single-handedly prevented us from getting out of student debt or affording a mortgage). It will always be easier to blame a younger generation than it is to imagine an end of capitalism. "Millennials don't have one thing to protest; we have a whole way of life," as journalist and critic Malcolm Harris suggests, reflecting on Occupy Wall Street as an "attempt to protest the whole knot." In *Kids These Days*, which tells the history of the "making of millennials," Harris defines generations as a form of crisis: "Wars, revolutions, market crashes, shifts in the mode of production, transformations in social relations: these are the things generations are made of." While these crises are continual, the idea of a generation creates social divisions that obstruct solidarity, which enables us to endure this relentlessness. Generations "look at each other not over a line, but over a gap," as Harris puts it, and the "divisions are very real, even as they're also imaginary."[7]

Child liberation refuses these divisions. If the crises are ongoing, and shared by all of us, then we will need multigenerational struggles, but also non-generational thinking, in order to meet them head on. What would it take to engage with generations not as a source of division but as a horizon? This entails plunging into the word—"generation," to generate, as in bring forth—precisely as a utopian problem. "Utopia lies at the horizon," writes Uruguayan author Eduardo Galeano. "When I draw nearer by two steps, [utopia] retreats two steps. If I proceed ten steps forward, it swiftly slips ten steps ahead. No matter how far I go, I can never reach it. What, then, is the purpose of utopia? It is to cause us to advance."[8]

§

Perhaps, like anyone who neither squashes nor flees from the problem of utopia, I just sound idealistic, unreasonable, hysterical—or, if you'd rather, *childish.* There are risks to going any further.

To this day, Shulamith Firestone's 1970 manifesto *The Dialectic of Sex* remains one of the most audacious attempts to envision child liberation in any specific terms. Firestone's imprint is everywhere in this book. It was in *The Dialectic of*

Sex that I first encountered child liberation as something more than an empty gesture, if not a punch line. "Childhood is hell," as Firestone boldly pronounced: "Children are repressed at every waking minute." Firestone conceived of the oppression of women and children as "intertwined and mutually reinforcing in such complex ways that we will be unable to speak of the liberation of women without also discussing the liberation of children." While acknowledging that "many women are sick and tired of being lumped together with children," she argued that solidarity with children is essential to any revolutionary feminist struggle.[9]

The Dialectic of Sex is a wild, controversial, messy book, written over the course of a few months, during which Firestone was pushed out of the New York Radical Feminists, a group she'd founded with Anne Koedt the year before. It was the third group Firestone had helped to establish between 1967 and 1969—New York Radical Women, followed by Redstockings—both of which she left to form the next. This was the tumultuous context in which Firestone constructed this ambitious, unruly project, with polemical chapters on Marx and Engels, American feminism, Freud, racism, love, romance, patriarchy, cultural history, and child liberation—all culminating in a series of demands and speculations about what she calls the "ultimate revolution."

In the final pages of *The Dialectic of Sex*, Firestone envisions a "cybernetic communism," delineating four "minimal demands": (1) that child-bearing be taken over by technology, and child-rearing be diffused to society as a whole; (2) the economic independence and self-determination of all; (3) the complete integration of women and children into the larger society; and (4) sexual freedom and love. She sets out to specify the conditions of child liberation with remarkable precision. The fulfillment of these demands, she imagines, would look something like this: "The concept of childhood has been abolished, children having full political, economic, and sexual rights, their educational/ work activities no different from those of adults." In the absence of the "psychologically destructive genetic 'parenthood' of one or two arbitrary adults," children would "still form intimate love relationships, but instead of developing close ties with a decreed 'mother' and 'father', the child might now form those ties with people of his own choosing, of whatever age or sex," with the responsibility for their physical welfare spread across a larger number of people. "[All] adult-child relationships will have been mutually chosen—equal, intimate relationships free of material dependencies," she explains. Children "would mingle freely throughout the society to the benefit of all, thus satisfying that legitimate curiosity about the young which is often called the reproductive 'instinct.'"[10] Note the way her prose moves between tenses, bouncing from what *has* happened to what *would* happen to what *will have* been. What a dream to leap into—and what a treacherous set of questions it invites.

Throughout her last chapter, Firestone recognizes this account of the ultimate revolution as an exercise of making "some 'dangerous utopian' concrete proposals." Unabashedly, but not without awareness of "the peculiar failure of imagination concerning alternatives to the family," she portrays herself as drawing up a model "subject to the limitations of any plan laid out on paper by a solitary individual." Her proposal is "sketchy" and "meant to stimulate thinking in fresh areas rather than to dictate the action."[11] To the extent that she outlines a program, she asserts that *flexibility* is the most important characteristic of revolution.

When I first read *The Dialectic of Sex*, I was parenting (that is, *mothering*) a toddler, and Firestone's famous declaration that "pregnancy is barbaric" knocked me with full force. I disagreed with many aspects of her book, but I was also captivated by the tenacity of her writing, and by her vulnerability.[12]

Firestone had died the year before, in late August 2012, at the age of sixty-seven. The story of her death agonizes. She was found in her fifth-floor studio in the East Village by the building superintendent, who came in through the fire escape. Her rent bill had been sitting outside her door for days. When neighbors reported a smell in the building, they contacted the landlord. Her body was face down on the floor and had laid there for at least a week. Her studio was in disarray, even worse than usual. And there was no food in her kitchen—a detail that prompted much speculation. Did she starve? Was it suicide? How are we to understand what became of her life?

Much of Firestone's adult years were spent in and out of institutions, where she endured an assortment of medical treatments for psychological diagnoses, including schizophrenia. By the time *The Dialectic of Sex* was published in October 1970, she had already retreated from public life, at the age of twenty-five. That May, Firestone wrote a letter to her sister

Laya, in which she confessed, "I don't believe finally that the revolution is so imminent that it's worth tampering with my whole psychological structure." In the years that followed, there were stories of her being spotted in the East Village in disguise, sometimes calling herself by the name "Kathy." At one point, Laya flew to New York to discover her sister panhandling, "carrying a bag holding a hammer and an unopened can of food," as she later recalled.[13]

In an essay following Firestone's death featured in *The New Yorker*, feminist author Susan Faludi chronicles various efforts that were made to care for Firestone. A group called Friends of Shulamith Firestone was formed in 1989, after a local newspaper published a gossip column about how "the author of *The Dialectic of Sex* was acting crazy and was about to be evicted from her Second Street studio."[14] But Firestone was certain that the group was in fact conspiring against her, and perhaps responsible for the gossip column itself. Months later, she lost that apartment, and her belongings were consigned to the trash. Another support system formed in the early 1990s. In each of these support systems, we find instances of what might be understood as collective mothering—a kind of care that for Firestone, estranged from her own family, found challenging to receive. However, the latter attempt was more successful. Every week a group of women met with Firestone to help her with groceries and cleaning, and to make sure she was taking her antipsychotic medications. Often, it would seem, Firestone was held up by her feminist comrades, in spite of the ways she pushed them away, and the ways they were pulled apart by a broader culture of divisiveness.

Over the years, Firestone had stopped writing—or rather, she felt that she could no longer write. She did not publish another book until decades later, in 1998, with the help of her supporters. *Airless Spaces*, a collection of stories, draws from her time in mental institutions and encounters on the Lower East Side. "Airless space" was how she'd come to understand her life after *The Dialectic of Sex*—and coming out of hospitalization. She characterizes this as a state of "emotional paralysis," the title of one of her stories (and perhaps the most heartbreaking), in which she writes of herself in the third person.[15] At Firestone's memorial, Kate Millett read the following passage from this story:

> She could not read. She could not write . . . the words bounced off her forehead like it was steel; she simply couldn't care about the contents of any written material, be it heavy or lightweight. Why? Why read it? Why absorb it? . . . She was lucid, yes, but at what price. She sometimes recognized on the faces of others joy and ambition and other emotions she could recall having had once, long ago. But her life was ruined, and she had no salvage plan.[16]

That it was Millett who shared this passage feels especially poignant. Millett, the author of another groundbreaking feminist text, *Sexual Politics* (published only a few months before *The Dialectic of Sex*), was institutionalized multiple times as well, beginning in 1973. In *The Loony-Bin Trip*, written in 1990, Millett reflects on her experiences of being involuntarily committed: "I am telling you what happened to me," she explains in the original preface, "because the telling functions for me as a kind of exorcism, a retrieval and vindication of the self—the mind— through reliving what occurred. It is a journey many of us take. Some of us survive it intact, others only partially survive."[17] Firestone was certainly among the latter.

For years, I have dwelled on the story of Firestone, curious about (if not anxious over) the perils of thought—the suffering so often encountered in dreaming up that which this world makes so unthinkable. I have lost people to this. At times, I have lost myself too. But I also wonder if losing oneself is sometimes necessary, in the effort to imagine such a utopian possibility as child liberation.

§

The impulse to pathologize utopian inquiry cannot be avoided; it must be anticipated, and disarmed. The pathologization of utopian thought has a long history as a weapon of political repression. "The Utopians have always been maniacs and oddballs," as Fredric Jameson reminds us, which can be "readily enough explained by the fallen societies in which they had to fulfill their vocation."[18] Utopian thought is foolish: it is a matter of fooling around, sometimes tragically. Utopia is also a childish thought, where childishness is understood as a kind of madness.

For Ernst Bloch, who dedicated much of his philosophical life to this madness and its methods, utopian inquiry "slips off the rails in a paranoid way, indeed almost voluntarily succumbs to delusion."[19] Bloch conceived of this as a practice first learned in childhood with daydreaming. Unlike the night dream, the daydream is participatory; it can be cultivated. And while the night dream exists in a repressive past—where, as Freud maintains, "we find the child and the child's impulses still living on"—the daydream takes its concern in "an as far as possible unrestricted journey forward," Bloch writes, through images of a not-yet that are "phantasied into life and into the world."[20] In *Cruising Utopia*, queer theorist José Esteban Muñoz elaborates on Bloch's utopian daydreaming as a form of "collective temporal distortion"—a not-yet that "approaches like a crashing wave."[21] We might also think through this distortion as what literary scholar Elizabeth Freeman calls "temporal drag," a not-now existing "less in the psychic time of the individual than in the movement time of collective political fantasy."[22]

Between these variations of the not-yet and the not-now, I want to stretch toward the question of childish time, as a way to theorize childish utopianism. How might we pursue child liberation as way of messing with, distorting, and even taunting the tyranny of adult time—what is sometimes described as "no future"?

Childhood is so often conceived through a language of growth and delay. We tend to think vertically about childhood as "growing up." Of this movement upward—"toward full stature, marriage, work, reproduction, and the loss of childishness"— queer theorist Kathryn Bond Stockton calls us into "notions of the horizontal—what spreads sideways—or sideways and backwards—more than a simple thrust towards height and for-ward time." To engage with the question of the child is to "climb inside a cloud," as Stockton imagines it; it is an act that leads us, "in moments, to cloudiness and ghostliness surrounding chil-dren as figures in time."[23]

Perhaps what I have been conjuring here is a cloud, then, more than a science fiction. Clouds accumulate, then diffuse. Clouds drift, like daydreams. If only for a moment, a cloud blocks the sun. Everything looks and feels different. The air cools, the light changes, and the moment passes. Childish time is fleeting, playful, queer, sideways. It takes hold of the present, but never forever. And yet it always comes back. It might arrive as a jolt to the senses, temporarily disturbing the way things appear to always be. It might be messy, and sometimes murky.

But none of this is to suggest that child liberation can't also be made concrete. Before turning to the question of prac-tice, however, I want to stay with this childish utopianism as a way toward solidarity with children. Childish utopianism can help us to dream, and to understand dreaming as a way of knowing. Here we might look to what Hortense Spillers calls "self-knowing," an ethical practice she derives from reflections on childhood. For Spillers, self-knowing is about the possibili-ties of childish time: moving "back in the direction of a 'prior' moment" in order to move "forward with another set of com-petencies that originate, we might say, in the bone ignorance of curiosity, the child's gift for strange dreams of flying and bi-zarre, yet correct, notions about the adult bodies around her."[24] This knowing state of strange dreaming does not have to end in the way that childhood supposedly does. How many of us roam through the world in this state, its own kind of madness, of knowing that the world could be otherwise?

§

We need utopian problems to develop revolutionary practices. While child liberation invites us into the *not-yet* and *not-now*, a conjectural time and space of utopian longing, it also grounds us in the exigencies of the present. With children, we are immediately confronted with realities of care and everyday life. And solidarity is how we reckon with this.

Solidarity moves between different registers of utopian thought and revolutionary strategy, taking everyday practices of collective care as the foundation of our political power. Solidarity (from the Latin *solidus*) means "of strong, firm, or substantial nature or quality." Solidarity is muscular. It requires exercise, nurturing, and intention. It takes form in the connections we make across our differences. Transformative solidarity, as activists Astra Taylor and Leah Hunt-Hendrix write, "always entails a leap of faith." But this leap is not toward "a messiah [or] a promised land, be it a heavenly kingdom or a post-revolutionary utopia," they suggest. "Instead, it is about believing in other people."[25]

Transformative solidarity calls for a distinction between the "ally" and the "accomplice." Warning us of what they describe as the "ally industrial complex," Indigenous Action Media writes that "at some point there is a 'we,' and we most likely will have to work together."[26] For this reason, there is a political urgency in forming "mutual understandings that are not entirely antagonistic; otherwise, we may find ourselves, our desires, and our struggles to be incompatible." As they argue: "There are certain understandings that may not be negotiable. There are contradictions that we must come to terms with, and certainly we will do this on our own terms. . . . But we need to know who has our backs, or more appropriately: who is with us at our sides?" While the ally is "the first to bail . . . when shit goes down," the accomplice, by contrast, "[isn't] afraid to engage in uncomfortable, unsettling, and/or challenging debates or discussions."[27] Solidarity, in other words, must be built among accomplices.

Child liberation demands accomplices from the adult world. The adult/child relation cannot be confined to the power dynamics of parent/child, teacher/child, and cop/child. Yet the possibilities of other dynamics are relentlessly pushed out of view. So long as there are "adults," there will be "children": in this sense, child liberation and the abolition of adulthood go hand in hand.

We need historical examples to strengthen our thinking about how to make child liberation present in our everyday practices. These examples are not blueprints to be replicated; they are revolutionary experiments that help us develop methodological insights—insights that reveal partial openings and choke points to be collectively seized and instrumentalized. Sometimes, adults have managed to include children in social movements. Other times, children have organized autonomously. Here I look to instances of children actively cocreating political struggles with adult comrades.

The Free Breakfast for School Children began in Oakland, California, in January 1969, as a community project launched by the Black Panther Party to address food insecurity. Every morning, members would arrive at Free Breakfast sites, ranging from community centers and churches to more ad hoc locations, to prepare food for children to eat on their way to school. But the point wasn't just to help ready students for their days in the school system. Reflecting on her years spent running Free Breakfast in a Brownsville community center in Brooklyn, Miriam Ma'at-Ka-Re Monges explains that, in addition to feeding hundreds of children each day, "we also nourished their minds with Black History lessons as they ate their meals."[28] This pedagogical aspect of the project, she insists, was the most important part. We might think about this as a practice of deschooling society.

While framed in nonthreatening, if not harmless, terms as a community action to feed children, as historians Joshua Bloom and Waldo E. Martin Jr. suggest, "no aspect of the Black Panther program was of greater concern than the Free Breakfast for Children Program," precisely for how it "fostered widespread support for the Panthers' revolutionary politics."[29] The political threat of Free Breakfast was in how it generated a sense of revolutionary possibility while improving the lives of people in the community.

Free Breakfast for Children was part of a broader program of "survival pending revolution" developed by the Black Panthers between 1966 and 1982. Out of the sixty-five community programs they established, many were youth oriented (including pediatric clinics, liberation schools, school tutorial programs, youth training and development, and child development), but also youth organized (teen councils, teen programs, and the Intercommunal Youth Institute). Bobby Seale emphasized that these were not reform programs but revolutionary programs: "A reform program is set up by the existing exploitative system as an appeasing handout, to fool the people and to keep them quiet," he argued, whereas a revolutionary program is "set forth by revolutionaries, by those who want to change the existing system to a better one."[30] Along with meeting basic material needs for community members, these revolutionary programs were both experimental and pedagogical. The programs were attempts to learn together toward something not fully knowable—building collective power as a means of liberation. Bringing children and questions of care to the foreground was an essential lesson in revolutionary strategy.

This is the enduring lesson of the Oaxaca uprisings of 2006 as well. That summer, hundreds of barricades were created throughout the city of Oaxaca after police opened fire on a protest organized by teachers, who had been on strike for the last month. The Popular Assembly of the Peoples of Oaxaca (APPO) was established soon after, creating large democratic assemblies throughout the city. Children and youth were active in many aspects of the uprising. "On the barricades, new forms of anarchism [began] to appear," as activist Gustavo Esteva recalls: "Long sleepless nights provided the opportunity for extensive political discussions, which awakened in many young people a hitherto nonexistent or inchoate social consciousness."[31]

A key moment in the uprising came when thousands of women took over the Canal Nueve, the state television and radio station, on August 1. "[For] the first time in their lives women had a space autonomous from men," as writer Barucha Peller explains, and "they found that the authoritarian regime of the state and the economy extended into their experience of the social division of labor and everyday life in the home and with family."[32] Rather than preventing women's political participation, gendered labor was the foundation of what would come to be known as the Oaxaca Commune. Incited, after all, by a teacher's strike, the uprising was always about solidarity with children. But in refusing pressure, mostly from men in the movement, to return to the private household, the women of the commune brought forth revolutionary forms of sociality, education, and care for children of the barricades. Out of this radical disjuncture from the private household emerged a struggle based in *insurgent social reproduction*: what M. E. O'Brien defines as "the meeting of direct daily needs in the midst of extended mass protest," in which "all aspects of family life can be contested and remade."[33]

The barricades of Oaxaca broke open transformations of everyday political life, creating new conditions for youth autonomy and intergenerational solidarity. Some of this was forged through conflict. Months after the insurrection had ended, in February 2007, Oaxacan Voices Constructing Autonomy and Freedom (VOCAL) was formed, integrating youth activists and university students, along with Zapatistas and anarchists who wanted to operate outside of the electoral politics of the

APPO. But many wanted to work outside of the adult supremacist dynamics of the APPO as well. "We were really bothered
by what went on in the meetings, and we decided to have some
meetings of our own," as student activist Sonia Hinojosa explains: "In APPO they would say, 'Well, you are very young. You
don't have experience.'" After they started organizing meetings
for youth, she recalls, "we started to look at what we had got-
ten from the experience of 2006 and what else we could do."[34]
While in VOCAL, youth discovered ways to work together autonomously, but also to build solidarity with elders with shared
principles—those who also rejected electoralism and represen-
tational politics as the basis of political solidarity.

Revolutionary strategies for youth autonomy can also be
found throughout the history of the Peruvian movement of
working children. Today in Peru, at least a quarter of children
are part of the workforce, and there are estimates of up to 90
percent of youth performing informal work. The working children's movement began in 1976 and led to the formation of the
Movement of Working Children and Adolescents, Children of
Christian Workers (MANTHOC) in 1977. MANTHOC was
established with five "intuitions" about self-organization: that
they should be autonomous; that youth members be in charge
and act as representatives; that the organization serve as a tool
to support needs of the masses; that they take a national and
international structure; and that they develop a new methodology and pedagogy for adults and children to work together.[35]

Intergenerational solidarity has been vital to these Peruvian
youth-organized movements. Adult comrades, *colaboradores*,

work with youth organizers with the goal of horizontalism. In her remarkable book *The Kids Are in Charge*, youth studies scholar Jessica Taft includes numerous interviews with youth and colaboradores about principles of intergenerationality. "A *colaborador* has to show them that they are totally convinced that children and adolescents are social subjects," Luis explains, reflecting on his years as an adult in the movement: "The *colaborador* has to get rid of their own adultist perspectives and take on the challenge of changing the adult-centrism of the society." Juliana, another colaborador, elaborates this as a practice of co-learning: "[We collaborate] not just in doing things, but also in learning," she explains. "Because he is collaborating with me from his experiences, and he shares them with me, and so I continue to learn more, I continue to take in more of the reality of children today."[36] To be a colaborador— that is, an adult accomplice—means to relate with children on these horizontal terms.

The intergenerational horizontalism of the Peruvian working children's movement clarifies a politics of *critical age consciousness*, intrinsic to solidarity with children: "Without a critical perspective on age," Taft writes, "adults and kids would be much more likely to replicate hierarchical patterns of interaction, underestimating kids' capacities and limiting their authority and power." Crucially, there are mutual stakes to this process of undoing the concepts of "childhood" and "adulthood," as an integral aspect of revolutionary strategy: "Adults can't work in horizontal collaboration with kids unless they truly value children's capacities and insights, and children can't work in horizontal collaboration with adults unless they have confidence in their own contributions."[37]

Critical age consciousness is as much a matter of learning as it is a matter of unlearning. It requires, of all of us, childish ways of knowing. This means asking questions, however unanswerable. It means dreaming, playing, taking risks—and it starts from the awareness of what we could discover with and from each other. We can try things, and fail, and still learn from that failure. And the more we show up for one another, the more we can do together.

We should not have to be parents, family members, legal guardians, teachers, childcare workers, nurses, or social workers to be a part of children's lives. But finding other ways to relate to each other is not only challenging; it is extremely risky. Adult accomplices (and especially nonparents) are targeted in the most vicious ways. They are called child abusers, pedophiles, and all manner of horrible things—they get doxxed and are subjected to smear campaigns by fascists, who hope to ruin their lives, along with those of the children they support. We must anticipate and protect each other against these threats, which continue to get worse.

Of the moral panic currently targeting teachers and health care workers who support gender nonconforming children, writer and organizer Kay Gabriel offers a powerful political objective: "The task for people who care about the political success of both trans people and the working class is to manifest the political coalition that the right is already attempting to neutralize." Building such a coalition, as Gabriel suggests, will involve working with teachers and community members, and "activating the real but passive class resentment and moral fury that people experience in their daily lives and directing them into political structures with a credible plan to win."[38] Fascist targeting works through isolation and individuation. Every day, there are so many adults who risk their safety, employment, and much more by acting in solidarity with children, and the risks they bear as individuals must be transformed into collective ones.

§

In a world that makes even the thought of child liberation such a dangerous proposition, where do we begin?

Years ago, during a week at a political summer camp, I spent much of my time with a group of a dozen or so feminists, discussing how to create solidarity with survivors in our various political milieus. Many of us shared frustrations with the ways that our unions, organizations, and political spaces mishandled sexual violence. We observed patterns in the rhetoric that shut down these conversations and spoke of the ways survivors are routinely unheard, and often worse: they are made to feel unreasonable, emotional, crazy—yes, childish—so that they can be treated as not credible, unjustified, and suspicious. Each of us, in some way, had faced retaliation for attempts we'd made to confront any of these problems. While I found myself feeling disheartened, my friend seemed unscathed. At the end of the week, I asked her what she thought any of us could do.

Her response was exquisitely practical: start with friendship. Make a group of friends and learn how to take care of each other. Start there, but also, don't stop there. Make sure that's just the beginning of something. Show up to things together. Change things together. And keep going.

Among children, friendships offer a way to endure this adultist world together, and even to transform it. It would be easy to claim that children are simply (that is, *naturally*) better at making friends than adults, but they aren't. To suggest this is to fetishize children—it works along the same logic of imagined purity and innocence that I have tried to trouble in these pages. Many children do not have friends, and they suffer from this immensely. Most of the time, children depend on adults to have access to other children, along with the possibility of friendship and other forms of sociality. Supporting children as they create and nurture friendships is a concrete way for adults to build solidarity.

As the parent of a person who the world calls an "only" child, I'm sometimes asked why I didn't have another—isn't it lonely for this child? Childhood can indeed be lonely, regardless of whether one has siblings. While I owe no one an answer to this question, I'm stunned by the way there seems to be no other solution to the presumed isolation of "only" children than to give them a sibling. Besides trusting Z when they tell me they don't want siblings (only dogs and cats), what I can do is support their friendships. And supporting these friendships is how, in turn, I can create solidarity with young people in everyday life beyond my roles as parent or teacher: for

Z's friends, I can be a trusting and trustworthy adult; for their parents and caretakers, I can be an alternate emergency contact, a person who picks up and drops off, a host of afternoon hangouts and sleepovers, and much more. None of this is out of the ordinary, but it is often overlooked as the groundwork for building solidarity.

With friends, if they are so lucky, children share secrets and carve out space together for mutual understanding. These are often the first hints of something like autonomy, fleeting experiences between school and the family that can take place among children. Co-survival: this is how my best friend and I remember our relationship began. Whether as distant memories, or in experiences that feel incredibly present, and even reactivated by the relationships we sustain, we can take from these moments the raw materials of a better collective life. With our friends, briefly yet beautifully, we remake the world.

Yet friendships can also, however unwittingly, reproduce family traumas. Sometimes, as writer and organizer Alva Gotby observes, friendships "function as a source of emotional reproduction, which serves to shore up the very relationships that continually marginalize those friendships and posits them as less important than romantic love and family bonds."[39] With friends we can share our suffering—confiding in each other about partners, family members, coworkers, bosses—only to recuperate and uphold those conditions and relationships after all. For this reason, friendships require criticality and commitment. They ask us to be accountable to each other and ourselves, as the basis of much more. This is not a given but something to be developed and challenged as a practice. In positing a radical politics of friendship, Gotby describes "a more open form of relationality, which could potentially traverse generational boundaries as well as allow for more expansive constructions of intimacy."[40] This politics of friendship pursues a much-broader remodeling of caring relationships, outside of legal or biological frameworks, but also apart from ideologies of childhood and adulthood. Gotby turns to comradeship as a "new horizon of feeling," reorienting us away from privatized attachments, and toward our desire for solidarity.

While a politics of friendship should not be mistaken for a solution, it could help us get at something harder to imagine. It could illuminate how we might relate to crises that present themselves as inevitable—all the suffering that entangles us in this world. Friendship is one way we find solace from that suffering and, in some cases, actively push against it. "*Against* is bound to *trying*" as writer Lola Olufemi suggests. It is a revolutionary method, a utopian pursuit: "To try is to take the prospect of the future (now, then, to come) so seriously that we dedicate our lives to living in and with it."[41]

There is a word for what I have been writing toward. Like "mother," "commune" is both parts verb and noun. To commune: to communicate with, to be together with. The commune: what is shared. The commune is not a utopia; it is an insurgency, created in the sense that it must be continually recreated.

To be clear, what I am describing is not an intentional community, collective living situation, or temporary autonomous

zone. It is nothing short of an ever-expansionary social transformation. It is not an unreachable utopia but a process that,
through collective struggles, we catch glimpses of—ways of
living that we know could be ours.

Writing of the Paris Commune, French anarchist Élisée
Reclus described this as the emergent possibility of a new society: "Everywhere the word 'commune' was understood in
the largest sense, as referring to a new humanity, made up of
free and equal companions, oblivious to the existence of old
boundaries," and with the aim of "helping each other in peace
from one end of the world to the other."[42] Reclus's conception
of "commune" moves away from a territorial definition and toward a revolutionary praxis. From the Paris Commune, literary scholar Kristin Ross draws out what she calls a "disruptive
history," identifying the possibilities of "'solidarity in diversi-
ty' at a global level" being forged today in local instantiations.
Comprising various communal practices, the commune form
can be understood as both "staying in place and standing in the
way," as Ross writes, "creating pragmatic alternatives *in the here
and now*."[43] While rooted in the present, the commune is also a
site of speculation. In our conditions of rising fascism, climate
apocalypse, and capitalist crisis, we need speculation to rescue
from this hell our revolutionary desires, and to strengthen our
collective practices and political questions.

In this spirit, how do we imagine life for children of the
commune? In her book *Family Abolition*, M.E. O'Brien takes up
this question. Children of the commune, she imagines, could
move through a variety of living arrangements as they grow

up, including children-centered group housing, while remaining within proximity of the original group of adults who cared for them, who they "may identify as their parents." In turn, adults could live in heterogeneous close relationships and "may choose to raise children they gestate or within whom they have a biological relationship; or they may choose other arrangements; or they, their child, or those immediately in their life may change those arrangements as a child ages." Within the commune, if a child found their living situation intolerable, there would be adults living "interdependent with them and in social proximity who could observe the situation, intervene collectively if needed, and offer easily accessible alternative[s]."[44] Rather than as the disappearance or replacement of what we know as parental love, the commune could take form through a radical awakening of so many ways to love, outside structures of scarcity and coercion, and unbound from ideologies of ownership and possession.

We bump up against such possibilities only with experimentation, and sometimes with failure. Without mistaking such forms as the answer itself, we learn from attempts to work through our political questions and desires in living form. This is the possibility that scholars and coauthors Anna Feigenbaum, Fabian Frenzel, and Patrick McCurdy find in protest camps, as "laboratories of the politics of the commons."[45] As opposed to a demonstration or other forms of protest, the protest camp is fundamentally a site of social reproduction—what they describe as "re-creational infrastructure," practices including shelter and defenses, as well as mobile kitchens, toilets, medical facilities, and childcare that "create the camp as a 'world.'"[46] In some cases, the protest camp fades into the background as a place to retreat from action in the streets. In other cases, the camp appears more clearly as the center of protest, animating practices of care that are otherwise invisibilized and exploitative features of capitalist life. The camp may take the purpose of a barricade or blockade itself, as in the Standing Rock encampments of 2016–17. Or the camp may function as a center of organizing and political education, as in the Occupy Wall Street encampments of 2011–12. These camps are not idealized for achieving complete autonomy but, rather, understood for how they wield forms of collective care and galvanize our political imaginations.

Since the Occupy movement, which began in New York City's Zuccotti Park during my final weeks of pregnancy in September 2011, much of my political life has been dedicated to such re-creational infrastructure for and with children. Initially this was a matter of addressing the absence of childcare at meetings, direct actions, and organizing spaces. I held meetings and trainings, created spreadsheets and resources, brought supplies. But I soon realized that childcare was not enough. Often it required separating children from the "real" political work being done, in another room or in a corner, to do activities that felt like missed opportunities for cultivating political solidarity. I also came to realize that this could not be resolved through inclusion alone—though bringing children who desire inclusion into otherwise adult-centered spaces is certainly an important strategy, this does not build from below conditions in which children can create political power together and potentially autonomously.

More and more, I became interested in approaching what we sometimes call "childcare" as something more like a protest camp: organized by adults and children together, and taking seriously the politics of play, care, education, and collaboration. Sometimes this looks like skillshares and workshops led or requested by children; activities that contribute to social movements such as political posters and banners; theater productions and musical performances; collective writing and discussions; sharing meals and ideas; or self-organized field trips, hikes, and bike rides.

Over the course of five years, we learned a lot from our experiences helping to organize a political summer camp—the same camp where my friend shared her thinking about the politics of friendship. The first year, Z was three years old, and the two of us caught a ride to the camp after a late invitation. When we arrived, I discovered that despite some discussion of childcare in the planning, there were no other young children there. A few people came together to quickly strategize how to support us. Every day, Z had adventures, explored the woods, swam in the river, made art and read stories, and each night they snuggled with me in a tent. In many ways, it was a beautiful experience. But I also understood why some of the parents who attended without their children had no plans to bring them in future years. The childcare was too ad hoc, and isolated. Still, it had been a remarkable experiment. A year later, Z and I brought my partner to the camp, and we invited other children and caretakers to join us. We spent the months ahead planning children's activities with a few people Z and I had met the summer before, most of whom were not parents but adults committed to principles of mutual aid, including childcare and eldercare. Each subsequent year, the children's component of the camp improved. It wasn't perfect, but we learned important lessons with each attempt. Most of all, it brought forth a political life that Z and I have nurtured together since, and in solidarity.

A few years later, some of the people who had dedicated themselves to working on children's experiences of the camp came together to organize a new version, this time entirely centered on children. We began planning with a group of people—a mix of legally recognized parents or guardians, "bonus parents" and caretakers, childcare workers and teachers—to make a kids' camp that involved about a dozen young people ranging from ages two to fifteen. The idea was that kids could make choices together throughout the camp with our support. At the end of the week, we committed to organizing for the next year, and to keep going.

These are the scraps of something bigger, much like the pages of this book. And perhaps that's all we have, between uprisings—moments when we come together and confront what we can't quite imagine on our own. What we discover in these experiments can never be a complete vision; yet the more we learn to question the logic of adult supremacy in our everyday lives, and to devise other ways of caring for children, the closer we get to the possibility of solidarity. To start, we can look at what we long for, together, and try for it. This essay was written against different ways of thinking about children that naturalize and legitimate their domination by adults, with the goal of finding ways to unthink adult power, rather than reinvent it. I never promised any solutions, but I hope what I've written can help with the grappling.

Just as the idea of children puts into crisis what we might think of adulthood, living in relation to children continually challenges what we understand as liberation. What children reveal to us, day to day, is the reality we all share. No one can be truly autonomous. We depend on each other. Children are particularly dependent upon adults in the way our lives together are organized. Adults give them access to shelter, food, clothing, medicine, transportation, education, and whatever might be defined as children's rights. But that dependence need not be one that reinforces adult domination and power. It need not be a relationship that stands in the way of how we might conceive of liberation. Anyone who has spent time with children knows that there are moments when it becomes necessary to intervene in a child's life and decision-making. In learning to live in this world, children sometimes put themselves or others into danger without realizing it. As do adults. Solidarity is not a matter of whether one intervenes, but how. These moments bare insights into how we can make decisions collectively and against the adult authoritarianism of "because I said so." An ethics of solidarity can only be developed through careful negotiation between dependency and responsibility. But this entails calling into question visions of liberation—for children, and all of us— and confronting our collective responsibility to the world.

Every day of sharing a life with children, it's hard to avoid confusion, frustration, anxiety, fear. In the absence of solidarity, wishing away these feelings may seem easier than trying to work through them. Child liberation is confounding to our political imagination and everyday lives, and it needs to be. It is a problem of thought, which demands a fundamental reworking of how we think and relate to each other. It is an invitation: as Le Guin implores of us, "Open your eyes . . . listen, listen."[47]

Acknowledgments

This book slowly emerged from time I've spent with young people who I'm honored to know and continue learning from: Abby, Adrian, Asia, Astrid, Autumn, Benj, Caleaf, Greta, Josie, Lazar, Leontine, Lily, Lorenzo, Lu, Makaia, Marcel, Maxine, Mila, MK, Noah, Raizel, Sasha, Teo, Wiley, and Xiola. Helen, Willa, and Tom: the questions of this book started with you long ago. And Ann, Anna, Ariel, Ash, Chloe, Clarice, Daniel, Guy, Hugh, Iris, Jackie, Jasper, Jen (both of you), Jessie, Josh (both of you), Jesse James, Justin, Kelly, Kim, Laura, Louis-Georges, Margot, Mark, Mars, Mia, Michelle, Nabel, Nadia, Neti, Penske, Ruth, Vanya, Yak—thank you for navigating so many of these questions together.

Throughout this process I've been anchored by some of my closest friends and co-thinkers: Alya Ansari, Sarah Brouillette, Marija Cetinic, Keegan Finberg, Max Fox, Jo Giardini, Brooke Lober, M. E. O'Brien, and Sean O'Brien, who provided feedback on drafts and much else; Johanna Isaacson, my forever collaborator; Samuel Catlin, Cole Cohen, Sidra Kamran, Phil Longo, Milo Muise, and Sheera Talpaz, with whom I've written alongside; E Conner, Dave Maher, and Kayte Terry, who helped me with research and made it fun; Taylor Eggan, Angus Reid, Kenan Bezhat Sharpe, and Sloane, who showed up when

I needed it at various points along the way; Charmaine Chua, Annie McClanahan, and Wendy Trevino, whose solidarity at the end I won't forget; my dogs Stella and Mona, who took me on morning and afternoon walks, and my cats Mega and Cosmo, who slept beside me at my desk.

There are many more friends and accomplices who made an imprint on what I've tried, at least, to put to page: Hope Barnes, Andy Battle, Barms, Hunter Bivens, Andrew Brooks, Chris Chen, Amy De'Ath, Shinjini Dey, Carl Diehl, Kendra Dority, Matthew Ellis, Malcolm Harris, Maggie Hennefeld, Justin Hogg, Malav Kanuga, Alírio Karina, Dominick Knowles, Kyle Kubler, Leigh Claire La Berge, Natasha Lennard, Eli Lichtenstein, Shawna Lipton, Astrid Lorange, Rowan McNamara, Kevin Miller, Chloe Minervini, Magally Miranda, Julian Francis Park, Gabriela Salvidea, Zach Schwartz-Weinstein, Wilson Sherwin, David Shulman, Chip Sinton, Eric Sneathen, Oki Sogumi, Juliana Spahr, Cassandra Troyan, Tyler Walicek, and Hannah Zeavin. To Flora Arnold, Hali Autumn, Vienna D'Angelo, Lauren Hough, Alex Neal, Kaya Noteboom, Tareeda Phirakulsiri, and Ryan Tardiff—thank you for helping me remember what we want from school. To my parents, my grandma, my cousins, and to Anna, Eric, Gabriel, Tessa, and Cheryl—I appreciate your patience and understanding. I must also thank Sophie Lewis, for encouraging me to write this book through years of writing around and sometimes away from it; my editor, Katy O'Donnell, for asking me to finally do it; and Sam Smith and Jameka Williams at Haymarket Books, for their enduring support.

During my final weeks of copy-editing this manuscript, we lost Joshua Clover, whom I am grateful to have known as a mentor, dear friend, and comrade. With much else, I'll carry this forward: "Nothing is over, that is the only certainty. The other certainty is that everything ends, even this."

C, I miss you, and M, I miss you too.

Lastly, my love to Jasmine Bridges, with whom I continue to survive childhood; to Kyle, for all the things I didn't believe were possible; and most of all to Zinnia, for absolutely everything.

Notes

Introduction: A World Against Children

1. Alice Speri, "Israel Responds to Hamas Crimes by Ordering Mass War Crimes in Gaza," *The Intercept*, October 9, 2023, https://theintercept.com/2023/10/09/israel-hamas-war-crimes-palestinians/.

2. "Photos: Grief in Gaza and the Loss of a Child," *Al Jazeera*, November 3, 2023, https://www.aljazeera.com/gallery/2023/11/3/photos-a-picture-and-its-story-grief-in-gaza-and-the-loss-of-a-child.

3. Lydia Polgreen, "This Photograph Demands an Answer," *New York Times*, November 13, 2023, https://www.nytimes.com/2023/11/13/opinion/gaza-war-children-photo.html.

4. Kathleen Kingsbury, "Opinion Today: When to Show War's Horrors," *New York Times*, November 13, 2023, https://www.nytimes.com/2023/11/13/opinion/nyt-opinion-photo-palestinian-children.html.

5. Polgreen, "This Photograph Demands an Answer."

6. "White House Walks Back Biden's Claim He Saw Children Beheaded by Hamas," *Al Jazeera*, October 12, 2023, https://www.aljazeera.com/news/2023/10/12/white-house-walks-back-bidens-claim-he-saw-children-beheaded-by-hamas.

7. Joshua Nelken-Zitser, "IDF Says It Won't Back up Its Claim That Hamas Decapitated Babies in Israel Because It Is 'Disrespectful for the Dead,'" *Business Insider*, October 11, 2023, https://www.businessinsider.com/idf-says-wont-back-up-beheaded-babies-disrespectful-2023-10.

8. Joseph Krauss and Wafaa Shurafa, "Israel's Opposing Factions Form Unity Government to Oversee War Sparked by Hamas

Attack," *PBS News*, October 11, 2023, https://www.pbs.org/newshour/world/israels-opposing-factions-form-unity-government-to-oversee-war-sparked-by-hamas-attack.

9. Jackie Wang, "Against Innocence: Race, Gender, and the Politics of Safety," *Lies Journal*, 2012, 167, https://www.liesjournal.net/volume1-10-againstinnocence.html.

10. Gia M. Badolato et al., "Racial and Ethnic Disparities in Firearm-Related Pediatric Deaths Related to Legal Intervention," *Pediatrics* 146, no. 6 (2020).

11. Aric Jenkins, "Jeff Sessions: Parents and Children Illegally Crossing the Border Will Be Separated," *Time*, May 7, 2018, https://time.com/5268572/jeff-sessions-illegal-border-separated/.

12. Tal Kopan, "DHS: 2,000 Children Separated from Parents at Border," *CNN*, June 15, 2018, https://www.cnn.com/2018/06/15/politics/dhs-family-separation-numbers/index.html.

13. Nomaan Merchant, "Hundreds of Children Wait in Border Patrol Facility in Texas," *AP News*, June 18, 2018, https://apnews.com/article/9794de32d39d4c6f89fbefaea3780769.

14. Camilo Montoya-Galvez, "U.S. Border Agents Are Separating Migrant Children from Their Parents to Avoid Overcrowding, Inspector Finds," *CBS News*, September 16, 2023, https://www.cbsnews.com/news/migrant-children-separated-parents-u-s-border-agents-overcrowding/.

15. Susan Sontag, *On Photography* (New York: Picador, 2010), 4, 14.

16. Sontag, *On Photography*, 20.

17. Steven Salaita, "Scrolling Through Genocide," *Steve Salaita* (blog), December 10, 2023, https://stevesalaita.com/scrolling-through-genocide/.

18. Susan Sontag, *Regarding the Pain of Others* (New York: Picador, 2013), 10.

19. Sontag, *Regarding the Pain of Others*, 9.

20. Yasmin El-Rifae, "To Know What They Know," *Parapraxis*, November 2024, https://www.parapraxismagazine.com/articles/to-know-what-they-know.

21. V. I. Lenin, "'Left-Wing' Communism: An Infantile Disorder," in *Lenin Collected Works*, vol. 31, *April - December 1920* (Moscow: Progress Publishers, 1966), 117–18.

22. Mao Tse-Tung, *Selected Works of Mao Tse-Tung*, vol. 6 (Paris: Foreign Languages Press, 2021), 307.

23. Murray Bookchin, *Social Anarchism or Lifestyle Anarchism: The Unbridgeable Chasm* (Edinburgh and San Francisco: AK Press, 1995), 7.

24. "RADICAL REDUX," *Chicago Tribune*, November 16, 1990, https://www.chicagotribune.com/1990/11/16/radical-redux/.

25. Luisa Neubauer et al., "Open Letter from Greta Thunberg: #FaceTheClimateEmergency," *Climate Emergency Declaration*, July 16, 2020, http://climateemergencydeclaration.org/open-letter-from-greta-thunberg-facetheclimateemergency/.

26. Kathi Weeks, *The Problem with Work: Feminism, Marxism, Antiwork Politics, and Postwork Imaginaries* (Durham: Duke University Press, 2011), 176.

27. "Over 330 Million Children Worldwide Living in Extreme Poverty," *UN News*, September 13, 2023, https://news.un.org/en/story/2023/09/1140687.

28. Nina Lakhani and Aliya Uteuova, "One in Four Faced Food Insecurity in America's Year of Hunger, Investigation Shows," *Guardian*, April 14, 2021, https://www.theguardian.com/environment/2021/apr/14/americas-year-of-hunger-how-children-and-people-of-color-suffered-most; "Violence against Children," World Health Organization, November 20, 2022, https://www.who.int/news-room/fact-sheets/detail/violence-against-children.

29. Sean Coughlan, "2018 'Worst Year for US School Shootings,'" *BBC News*, December 11, 2018, https://www.bbc.com/news/business-46507514; David Reidman, "How Many School Shootings? All Incidents From 1966–Present," K-12 School Shooting Database, accessed December 11, 2024, https://k12ssdb.org/all-shootings.

30. Delaney Tarr, "The Kids Shouldn't Have to Save Us," *Teen Vogue*, December 7, 2022, https://www.teenvogue.com/story/delaney-tarr-youth-gun-violence-activists-december-2022-special-issue.

31. "About," Moms for Liberty, accessed January 5, 2025, https://www.momsforliberty.org/about/.

32. Anna Skinner, "Man Stops Track Meet to Accuse 9-Year-Old

Girl of Being Transgender," *Newsweek,* June 13, 2023,
https://www.newsweek.com/man-accuses-9-year-old-girl-
transgender-1806369.

33. Summer Lin, Andrew J. Campa, and Howard Blume, "Fight Erupts
    at Anti-Pride Day Protest Outside L.A. School Where Trans
    Teacher's Flag Was Burned," *Los Angeles Times,* June 2, 2023,
    https://www.latimes.com/california/story/2023-06-02/parents-
    protest-lgbtq-pride-day-los-angeles-saticoy-elementary-school.

34. Amy Norton, "Suicide Rates Among U.S. Adolescents Doubled
    in 10 Years," *US News,* May 1, 2023, https://www.usnews.com/
    news/health-news/articles/2023-05-01/suicide-rates-among-
    u-s-adolescents-doubled-in-10-years.

35. Laura G. Fleszar et al., "Trends in State-Level Maternal Mor-
    tality by Racial and Ethnic Group in the United States," *JAMA*
    330, no. 1 (2023): 52, https://doi.org/10.1001/jama.2023.9043.

36. Tracey Wilkinson, Julie Maslowsky, and Laura Lindberg, "A
    Major Problem for Minors: Post-Roe Access to Abortion,"
    STAT, June 26, 2022, https://www.statnews.com/2022/06/26/
    a-major-problem-for-minors-post-roe-access-to-abortion/.

37. Solcyré Burga, "How a 10-Year-Old Rape Victim Who Traveled
    for an Abortion Became Part of a Political Firestorm," *Time,*
    July 15, 2022, https://time.com/6198062/rape-victim-10-abor-
    tion-indiana-ohio/; Lauren Aratani, "Girl, 13, Gives Birth after
    She Was Raped and Denied Abortion in Mississippi," *Guardian,*
    August 14, 2023, https://www.theguardian.com/world/2023/
    aug/14/mississippi-abortion-ban-girl-raped-gives-birth.

38. carla joy bergman, "Introduction," *Trust Kids!: Stories on Youth
    Autonomy and Confronting Adult Supremacy,* ed. carla joy berg-
    man, (Oakland: AK Press, 2022), 9.

39. Governor Greg Abbott to Commissioner Jaime Masters, Febru-
    ary 22, 2022, https://gov.texas.gov/uploads/files/press/
    O-MastersJaime202202221358.pdf.

40. Jules Gill-Peterson, *Histories of the Transgender Child* (Minne-
    apolis: University of Minnesota Press, 2018), 197.

41. Gill-Peterson, *Histories,* 4.

42. Max Fox, "The Traffic in Children," *Parapraxis,* December
    2022, https://www.parapraxismagazine.com/articles/the-
    traffic-in-children.

43. Claudia Rankine, "The Condition of Black Life Is One of Mourning," in *The Fire This Time: A New Generation Speaks about Race*, ed. Jesmyn Ward (New York: Scribner, 2016), 145.

44. Rankine, "The Condition of Black Life," 145.

45. Trina Greene Brown, *Parenting for Liberation: A Guide for Raising Black Children* (New York: The Feminist Press, 2020), 10.

46. Adrienne Cecile Rich, *Of Woman Born: Motherhood as Experience and Institution* (New York: W.W. Norton, 1976), 11.

47. "'Israel Is Starving Us' – Gaza Children Hold Press Conference at Al-Shifa Hospital (VIDEO)," *Palestine Chronicle*, November 7, 2023, https://www.palestinechronicle.com/israel-is-starving-us-gaza-children-hold-press-conference-at-al-shifa-hospital/.

48. Nadia Bou Ali, "Ugly Enjoyment: Affirming Life, Inconsolably," *Parapraxis*, November 2024, https://www.parapraxismagazine.com/articles/ugly-enjoyment.

1. Dreams Called Childhood

1. Sigmund Freud, *The Interpretation of Dreams* (1899; repr., Ware: Wordsworth Editions, 2014), 92.

2. Kathryn Bond Stockton, *The Queer Child, or Growing Sideways in the Twentieth Century* (Durham: Duke University Press, 2009), 30.

3. Jules Gill-Peterson, "The Child," *Parapraxis*, December 2022, https://www.parapraxismagazine.com/articles/the-child.

4. Philippe Ariès, *Centuries of Childhood: A Social History of Family Life*, trans. Robert Baldick (New York: Vintage, 1962).

5. Ariès, *Centuries of Childhood*, 411.

6. Paul B. Newman, *Growing Up in the Middle Ages* (Jefferson, NC, and London: McFarland & Co., 2007), 21–22.

7. Ariès, *Centuries of Childhood*, 40.

8. Hugh Cunningham, "Histories of Childhood," *American Historical Review* 103, no. 4 (October 1998): 1207, https://doi.org/10.2307/2651207.

9. Ariès, *Centuries of Childhood*, 412.

10. Michel de Montaigne, Michael Andrew Screech, and Michel de Montaigne, *The Complete Essays* (London and New York: Penguin Books, 1993), 53.

11. John Locke, *An Essay Concerning Human Understanding*, abr., ed. Kenneth P. Winkler (Indianapolis and Cambridge: Hackett, 1996), 33.

12. Thomas Hobbes, *Leviathan*, ed. Marshall Missner (1651; repr., New York: Pearson Longman, 2008), 66.

13. Immanuel Kant, *On Education* (1803; repr., Newburyport: Dover Publications, 2012), 55–56.

14. Jean-Jacques Rousseau, *Rousseau's Émile; or, Treatise on Education*, trans. William Harold Wayne (New York: D. Appleton and Co., 1892), 7, https://catalog.hathitrust.org/Record/100787637.

15. Rousseau, *Rousseau's Émile*, 4.

16. William Wordsworth and Samuel Taylor Coleridge, *Lyrical Ballads: With a Few Other Poems*, ed. Michael Schmidt (1798; repr., London: Penguin, 2006), 56.

17. Nancy Armstrong, *Desire and Domestic Fiction: A Political History of the Novel* (New York: Oxford University Press, 2006), 106.

18. Mary Wollstonecraft, *Thoughts on the Education of Daughters: With Reflections on Female Conduct in the More Important Duties of Life* (1787; repr., Clifton, NJ: A. M. Kelley, 1972), 103.

19. Wollstonecraft, *Thoughts on the Education of Daughters*, 3–5.

20. Ariès, *Centuries of Childhood*, 133.

21. Friedrich Engels, "Origins of the Family, Private Property, and the State (1884)," in *Marx/Engels Selected Works*, vol. 3 (London: Lawrence & Wishart, 1975).

22. Thomas Jefferson, "Founders Online: Thomas Jefferson to John Wayles Eppes, 30 June 1820," US National Archives and Records Administration, http://founders.archives.gov/documents/Jefferson/03-16-02-0052.

23. Steven Mintz, "Children in North American Slavery," in *The Routledge History of Childhood in the Western World*, ed. Paula S. Fass (London and New York: Routledge, Taylor & Franci, 2015).

24. Hortense J. Spillers, "Mama's Baby, Papa's Maybe: An American Grammar Book," *Diacritics* 17, no. 2 (1987): 74, https://doi.org/10.2307/464747.

25. Tony C. Brown, *Statelessness: On Almost Not Existing* (Minneapolis and London: University of Minnesota Press, 2022).

26. "List of Goods Produced by Child Labor or Forced Labor," US

Department Of Labor, 17–25, accessed January 5, 2025, https://www.dol.gov/agencies/ilab/reports/child-labor/list-of-goods.

27. "Child Labor in the United States," American Federation of Teachers, June 16, 2014, https://www.aft.org/community/child-labor-united-states.

28. International Labour Organisation and UNICEF, eds., *Child Labour: Global Estimates 2020, Trends and the Road Forward* (New York: ILO and UNICEF, 2021).

29. "Violence Against Children," World Health Organization, November 29, 2022, https://www.who.int/news-room/fact-sheets/detail/violence-against-children.

30. "Child Maltreatment," World Health Organization, November 5, 2024, https://www.who.int/news-room/fact-sheets/detail/child-maltreatment.

31. "National Statistics on Child Abuse," National Children's Alliance, accessed January 3, 2025, https://www.nationalchildrensalliance.org/media-room/national-statistics-on-child-abuse/; US Department of Health & Human Services, *Child Maltreatment 2022*, January 29, 2024, https://www.acf.hhs.gov/cb/data-research/child-maltreatment.

32. K. D. Griffiths and J. J. Gleeson, "Kinderkommunismus: A Feminist Analysis of the 21st Century Family and a Communist Proposal for its Abolition," *A New Institute for Social Research* (2015), https://www.isr.press/Griffiths_Gleeson_Kinderkommunismus/index.html.

33. Exec. Order No. 14187, "Protecting Children From Chemical and Surgical Mutilation," January 28, 2025, https://www.whitehouse.gov/presidential-actions/2025/01/protecting-children-from-chemical-and-surgical-mutilation/.

34. Rebekah Sheldon, *The Child to Come: Life after the Human Catastrophe* (Minneapolis: University of Minnesota Press, 2016), 37.

35. Joseph Zornado, *Inventing the Child* (Hoboken: Taylor and Francis, 2006), xviii.

36. June Jordan, "The Creative Spirit: Children's Literature," in *Revolutionary Mothering: Love on the Front Lines*, ed. Alexis Pauline Gumbs, China Martens, and Mai'a Williams (Oakland, CA: PM Press, 2016), 17–18.

37. Jacob Grimm and Wilhelm Grimm, *The Complete Grimm's Fairy*

Tales (New York: Pantheon, 2005), 534–35.

38. D. W. Winnicott, "The Theory of the Parent-Infant Relationship," in *Essential Papers on Object Relations*, ed. Peter Buckley, Essential Papers in Psychoanalysis (New York: New York University Press, 1986), 41.

39. Winnicott, "Parent-Infant Relationship," 41.

40. Sara Ahmed, *Willful Subjects* (Durham: Duke University Press, 2014), 63.

41. Gayatri Spivak, "Can the Subaltern Speak?," in *Colonial Discourse and Post-Colonial Theory: A Reader*, ed. Patrick Williams and Laura Chrisman (London: Routledge, 2013), 92.

42. Spivak, "Can the Subaltern Speak?," 102–4.

43. Rudyard Kipling, *The Jungle Book* (New York: The Century Company, 1920), 6.

44. Kipling, *The Jungle Book*, 17, 131.

45. Frantz Fanon, *Black Skin, White Masks*, rev. ed. (New York: Grove, 2008), 124.

46. Edward Said, "Jungle Calling: Johnny on Weissmuller's Tarzan," in *Film Theory: Critical Concepts in Media and Cultural Studies*, vol. 1, ed. Andrew Utterson, K. J. Shepherdson, and Philip Simpson (London: Routledge, 2004), 398.

47. Fanon, *Black Skin, White Masks*, 131, 125.

48. J. M. Barrie, *Peter and Wendy* (Leipzig: Bernhard Tauchitz, 1911), 159.

49. Barrie, *Peter and Wendy*, 107, 82.

50. Jacqueline Rose, *The Case of Peter Pan; Or, The Impossibility of Children's Fiction* (Philadelphia: University of Pennsylvania Press, 1992), 1.

51. Rose, *The Case of Peter Pan*, 13.

52. Rose, *The Case of Peter Pan*, 67.

53. Gilles Deleuze, *Desert Islands and Other Texts, 1953-1974*, ed. David Lapoujade, trans. Mike Taormina (Los Angeles: Semiotext(e), 2004), 10.

54. Jordan, "The Creative Spirit," 17–18.

55. Gabrielle Owen, *A Queer History of Adolescence: Developmental Pasts, Relational Futures* (Athens: University of Georgia Press, 2020), 32.

56. Owen, *Queer History of Adolescence*, 44.

57. Michel Foucault, *The History of Sexuality*, ed. Frédéric Gros, trans. Robert Hurley (New York: Vintage, 1990), 42–44.

58. Owen, *Queer History of Adolescence*, 7.

59. Oscar Wilde, *The Picture of Dorian Gray* (New York, 1909), 28, 244.

60. Vladimir Nabokov, *Lolita*, Large print ed. (Thorndike, ME: G. K. Hall, 1997), 19, 16–17.

61. Ben Cosgrove, "The Invention of Teenagers: LIFE and the Triumph of Youth Culture," *TIME*, September 28, 2013, https://time.com/3639041/the-invention-of-teenagers-life-and-the-triumph-of-youth-culture/.

62. Erik H. Erikson, *Childhood and Society* (W. W. Norton & Company, 1993), 261.

63. Anna Freud, *Normality and Pathology in Childhood: Assessments of Development* (London: Karnac Books, 1989), 105

64. Tiqqun, *Preliminary Materials for a Theory of the Young-Girl*, trans. Ariana Reines (Los Angeles: Semiotext(e), 2012), 101.

65. Tiqqun, *Preliminary Materials*, 129.

66. Sara Austin, *Monstrous Youth: Transgressing the Boundaries of Childhood in the United States* (Columbus: Ohio State University Press, 2022), 8.

67. Karen J. Renner, *Evil Children in the Popular Imagination* (New York: Palgrave Macmillan, 2016), 153.

2. On the Possibility of Mothering

1. Jacqueline Rose, *Mothers: An Essay on Love and Cruelty* (New York: Farrar, Straus & Giroux, 2019), 2, 188, 1.

2. Alexis Pauline Gumbs, "m/other ourselves: a Black queer feminist genealogy for radical mothering," *Revolutionary Mothering: Love on the Front Lines*, ed. Alexis Pauline Gumbs, China Martens, and Mai'a Williams (Oakland: PM Press, 2016), 21.

3. Gumbs, "m/other ourselves," 23.

4. Adrienne Cecile Rich, *Of Woman Born: Motherhood as Experience and Institution* (New York: W.W. Norton, 1976), 280.

5. Audre Lorde, *I Am Your Sister: Collected and Unpublished Writings of Audre Lorde*, ed. Rudolph P. Byrd, Johnnetta B. Cole, and Beverly Guy-Sheftall (Oxford: Oxford University Press, 2009), 207.

6. Christina Elizabeth Sharpe, *In the Wake: On Blackness and Being* (Durham: Duke University Press, 2016), 78.

7. Angela Y. Davis, *Women, Race, and Class* (New York: Vintage, 1983), 7.

8. Delores M. Walters, "Re(Dis)Covering and Recreating the Cultural Milieu of Margaret Garner," in *Gendered Resistance: Women, Slavery, and the Legacy of Margaret Garner*, ed. Mary E. Frederickson and Delores M. Walters (Urbana: University of Illinois Press, 2013), 9.

9. Mark Reinhardt, *Who Speaks for Margaret Garner?* (Minneapolis: University of Minnesota Press, 2010), 31–32.

10. Toni Morrison, *Beloved*, 1st ed. (New York: Alfred A. Knopf, 1987), 236.

11. Spillers, "Mama's Baby, Papa's Maybe," 80.

12. Morrison, *Beloved*, 242, 324.

13. Morrison, *Beloved*, 281, 297.

14. Audre Lorde, *Sister Outsider: Essays and Speeches* (Berkeley, CA: Crossing Press, 2007), 157–58, 166.

15. Morrison, *Beloved*, 297.

16. Morrison, *Beloved*, 308.

17. Silvia Federici, *Revolution at Point Zero: Housework, Reproduction, and Feminist Struggle*, 2nd ed. (Oakland: PM Press, 2020), 11.

18. Federici, *Revolution at Point Zero*, 12.

19. Federici, *Revolution at Point Zero*, 21, 17.

20. Mariarosa Dalla Costa and Selma James, *The Power of Women and the Subversion of the Community*, 3rd ed. (Bristol: Falling Wall Press, 1975), 24, 26.

21. Dalla Costa and James, 26, 27.

22. Dalla Costa and James, 13.

23. Davis, *Women, Race, and Class*, 237, 238.

24. bell hooks, *Feminist Theory: From Margin to Center*, 2nd ed. (Cambridge, MA: South End Press, 2000), 133.

25. hooks, *Feminist Theory*, 133.

26. Sophie Lewis, *Full Surrogacy Now: Feminism Against Family* (London: Verso, 2019), 26.

27. Lewis, *Full Surrogacy Now*, 168.

28. Lewis, *Full Surrogacy Now*, 48.

29. Celeste Ng, *Little Fires Everywhere* (New York: Penguin, 2017), 213.

30. Ng, *Little Fires Everywhere*, 213.

31. Ng, *Little Fires Everywhere*, 214.

32. Lewis, *Full Surrogacy Now*, 19–20.

33. bell hooks, *Feminism Is for Everybody: Passionate Politics*, 2nd ed. (Hoboken: Taylor & Francis, 2014), 74.

34. *Shoplifters*, dir. Hirokazu Koreeda (AOI Promotion, Fuji Television Network, Gaga, 2018), 121 min.

35. "Breastfeeding FAQs: How Much and How Often (for Parents)," Nemours Kids Health, accessed January 4, 2025, https://kidshealth.org/en/parents/breastfeed-often.html.

36. Jill Radtke Demirci et al., "Breastfeeding and Short Sleep Duration in Mothers and 6–11-Month-Old Infants," *Infant Behavior and Development* 35, no. 4 (December 2012): 884–86, https://doi.org/10.1016/j.infbeh.2012.06.005.

37. M. E. O'Brien, *Family Abolition: Capitalism and the Communizing of Care* (London: Pluto Press, 2023), 56–57.

38. I write more extensively about Lewis's work in Madeline Lane-McKinley, "Unthinking the Family in 'Full Surrogacy Now,'" *Los Angeles Review of Books*, June 10, 2019, https://lareviewofbooks.org/article/unthinking-the-family-in-full-surrogacy-now/. I put her more recent book, *Abolish the Family*, into dialogue with O'Brien's *Family Abolition* in Madeline Lane-McKinley, "Beyond the End of the World: M. E. O'Brien's *Family Abolition*," *Protean Magazine*, September 29, 2023, https://proteanmagstaging.wpcomstaging.com/2023/09/29/beyond-the-end-of-the-world-m-e-obriens-family-abolition/.

39. Rose, *Mothers*, 199.

40. Simone de Beauvoir, *The Second Sex*, trans. Constance Borde and Sheila Malovany-Chevallier (1949; repr., New York: Vintage, 2011), 566.

41. de Beauvoir, *The Second Sex*, 566.

3. The Trouble with School

1. Eve L. Ewing, *Original Sins: The (Mis)education of Black and Native Children and the Construction of American Racism* (New York: Penguin Random House, 2025), 17, 21.

2. Exec. Order No. 14190, "Ending Radical Indoctrination in K-12

Schooling," January 29, 2025. https://www.whitehouse.gov/presidential-actions/2025/01/ending-radical-indoctrination-in-k-12-schooling/.

3. Francisco Ferrer Guardia et al., *Anarchist Education and the Modern School: A Francisco Ferrer Reader* (Oakland, CA: PM Press, 2019), 87, 99, 13.

4. Voltairine de Cleyre, *Exquisite Rebel: The Essays of Voltairine de Cleyre: Feminist, Anarchist, Genius*, ed. Sharon Presley and Crispin Sartwell (Albany, NY: State University of New York Press, 2010), 253–54.

5. de Cleyre, *Exquisite Rebel*, 264.

6. Federico Ferretti, "The Spatiality of Geography Teaching and Cultures of Alternative Education: The 'Intuitive Geographies' of the Anarchist School in Cempuis (1880–1894)," *Cultural Geographies* 23, no. 4 (2016): 620.

7. Kazuo Ishiguro, *Never Let Me Go* (New York: Vintage, 2006), 73.

8. Ishiguro, *Never Let Me Go*, 258.

9. Kim TallBear, *Native American DNA: Tribal Belonging and the False Promise of Genetic Science* (Minneapolis: University of Minnesota Press, 2013), 46.

10. Holly Littlefield, *Children of the Indian Boarding Schools* (Minneapolis: Carolrhoda Books, 2001), 15.

11. Nick Estes, "My Relatives Went to a Catholic School for Native Children. It Was a Place of Horrors," *Guardian*, June 30, 2021, https://www.theguardian.com/commentisfree/2021/jun/30/my-relatives-went-to-a-catholic-school-for-native-children-it-was-a-place-of-horrors.

12. Hilary Beaumont, "US Gov't: At Least 53 Burial Sites at Indigenous Boarding Schools," *Al Jazeera*, May 11, 2022, https://www.aljazeera.com/news/2022/5/11/us-govt-at-least-53-burial-sites-at-indigenous-boarding-schools.

13. Emma Goldman, "The Social Importance of the Modern School" (1910), available at https://theanarchistlibrary.org/library/emma-goldman-the-social-importance-of-the-modern-school.

14. Michel Foucault, *Discipline and Punish: The Birth of the Prison*, trans. Alan Sheridan, 2nd ed. (New York: Vintage, 1995), 141.

15. Andrew Scahill, *The Revolting Child in Horror Cinema: Youth Rebellion and Queer Spectatorship* (New York: Palgrave Macmillan, 2015), 5–6.

16. *If....*, dir. Lindsay Anderson (Memorial Enterprises, 1969) 1h 51 min.

17. Lindsay Anderson, *Never Apologise: Collected Writings*, ed. Paul Ryan (London: Plexus, 2005), 123.

18. I'm indebted to a few friends for helping me to research cultural representations of school, including E Conner, who introduced me to *Bambule*, as well as Dave Maher, Sean O'Brien, and Kayte Terry.

19. *Bambule*, dir. Eberhard Itzenplitz (West Germany, May 24, 1970), 90 min.

20. Michael Paulson, "Church Allowed Abuse by Priest for Years," *Boston Globe*, January 6, 2002, https://www.bostonglobe.com/news/special-reports/2002/01/06/church-allowed-abuse-priest-for-years/cSHfGkTIrAT25qKGvBuDNM/story.html.

21. David Lorenz, "In Support of SB575, by David Lorenz, Testimony before the Maryland Legislature, March 1, 2007," March 1, 2007, https://www.bishop-accountability.org/news5/2007_03_01_Lorenz_InSupport.htm.

22. *Associated Press*, "Missouri, Illinois, 31 Other States Exempt Clergy from Reporting Abuse," *Spectrum News*, September 28, 2022, https://spectrumlocalnews.com/mo/st-louis/news/2022/09/28/33-states-exempt-clergy-from-reporting-abuse.

23. "Catholic Schools and Parents Grapple with Whether to Address Abuse Report," NPR, September 6, 2018, https://www.npr.org/2018/09/06/644898991/back-to-school-for-catholic-students-in-pennsylvania-following-abuse-report.

24. Louisa Ewald, Claire Henson, and Emmanuela Gakidou, "COVID-Era Learning Loss Tied to Food Insecurity," Think Global Health, January 24, 2024, https://www.thinkglobal-health.org/article/covid-era-learning-loss-tied-food-insecurity.

25. Tom Kane and Sean Reardon, "Parents Don't Understand How Far Behind Their Kids Are in School," *New York Times*, May 11, 2023, https://www.nytimes.com/interactive/2023/05/11/opinion/pandemic-learning-losses-steep-but-not-permanent.html.

26. Robin L. West, "The Harms of Homeschooling," *Philosophy and Public Policy Quarterly* 29, no. 3/4 (2009), https://www.educacaodomiciliar.fe.unicamp.br/sites/www.educacaodomiciliar.fe.unicamp.br/files/2022-07/The%20Harms%20of%20Homeschooling.pdf.

27. Akilah Richards, *Raising Free People* (Oakland: PM Press, 2020), 14.

28. John Caldwell Holt, *Escape from Childhood* (New York: Ballantine, 1975), 2.

29. John Caldwell Holt, *Instead of Education: Ways to Help People Do Things Better* (Boulder, CO: Sentient Publications, 2004), 4.

30. John Caldwell Holt, *How Children Fail*, rev. ed (Reading, MA: Addison-Wesley Pub. Co, 1995), 263.

31. John Caldwell Holt, *Learning All the Time*, (Reading, MA: Addison-Wesley Pub. Co, 1991), 162.

32. Ivan Illich, *Deschooling Society* (1970; repr., London: Marion Boyars, 2002), 35, 72–73.

33. Illich, *Deschooling Society,* 35.

34. Illich, *Deschooling Society,* 35.

35. Samuel P. Catlin, "The Campus Does Not Exist: How Campus War Is Made," *Parapraxis,* August 2024, https://www.parapraxismagazine.com/articles/the-campus-does-not-exist.

36. Catlin, "The Campus Does Not Exist."

37. Daniel Spaulding, "On Hating Students," E-Flux Education, May 28, 2024, https://www.e-flux.com/education/features/610182/on-hating-students.

38. Sharon Zhang, "First-Ever Faculty Gaza Solidarity Encampment Erected at The New School," *Truthout,* May 8, 2024, https://truthout.org/articles/first-ever-faculty-gaza-solidarity-encampment-erected-at-the-new-school/.

39. Raoul Vaneigem, "A Warning to Students of All Ages," trans. JML, August 2000, available at https://theanarchistlibrary.org/library/a-warning-to-students-of-all-ages.

40. "Teenage Trans Activists Occupy Department for Education Headquarters in Protest for Safe, Inclusive Education for Trans Students," Trans Kids Deserve Better, August 23, 2024, https://transkidsdeservebetter.org/teenage-trans-activists-occupy-dfe-hq-in-for-trans-rights.

41. James Factora, "Trans Teens Are Occupying the U.K. Department for Education to Demand Policy Changes," *Them,* August 27, 2024, https://www.them.us/story/trans-kids-deserve-better-uk-department-of-education-encampment.

4. Child Liberation: A Utopian Problem

1. Ursula K. Le Guin, *The Dispossessed*, rev. ed. (New York: HarperCollins, 2024), xviii.
2. Le Guin, *The Dispossessed*, xix.
3. Octavia Butler, *A Few Rules for Predicting the Future* (San Francisco: Chronicle, 2024), 19.
4. Butler, *A Few Rules*, 55.
5. Kathi Weeks, *The Problem with Work: Feminism, Marxism, Antiwork Politics, and Postwork Imaginaries* (Durham: Duke University Press, 2011), 181.
6. Sam Leith, "The Lunacy of Child Liberation," *UnHerd*, April 30, 2024, https://unherd.com/2024/05/the-lunacy-of-child-liberation/.
7. Malcolm Harris, *Kids These Days: Human Capital and the Making of Millennials* (New York: Back Bay Books Little, Brown and Company, 2017), 3, 223.
8. Eduardo Galeano, "Window Utopia," in *Walking Words*, trans. Mark Fried (New York: W. W. Norton, 1997), 326.
9. Shulamith Firestone, *The Dialectic of Sex: The Case for Feminist Revolution* (New York: Farrar, Straus & Giroux, 2003), 93, 94, 65.
10. Firestone, *The Dialectic of Sex*, 214.
11. Firestone, *The Dialectic of Sex*, 203.
12. More of my critique of Firestone can be found in Madeline Lane-McKinley, "The Dialectic of Sex, after the Post-1960s," *Cultural Politics* 15, no. 3 (November 1, 2019): 331–42, https://doi.org/10.1215/17432197-7725479. Many thanks to Morgan Adamson and Sarah Hamblin for their editorial support.
13. Susan Faludi, "Death of a Revolutionary," *The New Yorker*, April 8, 2013, https://www.newyorker.com/magazine/2013/04/15/death-of-a-revolutionary.
14. Faludi, "Death of a Revolutionary."
15. Shulamith Firestone, *Airless Spaces* (London: Semiotext(e), 1998), 57.
16. Firestone, *Airless Spaces*, 57–59.
17. Kate Millett, *The Loony-Bin Trip* (Champaign: University of Illinois Press, 2000), 11.
18. Fredric Jameson, *Archaeologies of the Future: The Desire Called*

Utopia and Other Science Fictions (New York: Verso, 2005), 10.

19. Ernst Bloch, *The Principle of Hope*, vol. 3, trans. Neville Plaice, Stephen Plaice, and Paul Knight (Cambridge, MA: MIT Press, 1986), 473.

20. Sigmund Freud, *The Interpretation of Dreams* (1899; repr., Ware: Wordsworth Editions, 2014), 224; Ernst Bloch, "The Meaning of Utopia," in *Marxism and Art: Essays Classic and Contemporary*, ed. Maynard Solomon (Detroit: Wayne State University Press, 1979), 578.

21. José Esteban Muñoz, *Cruising Utopia: The Then and There of Queer Futurity* (New York: New York University Press, 2009), 1, 18, 185.

22. Elizabeth Freeman, *Time Binds: Queer Temporalities, Queer Histories* (Durham: Duke University Press, 2010), 65.

23. Kathryn Bond Stockton, *The Queer Child; or, Growing Sideways in the Twentieth Century* (Durham: Duke University Press, 2009), 2, 4.

24. Hortense J. Spillers, "'All the Things You Could Be by Now If Sigmund Freud's Wife Was Your Mother': Psychoanalysis and Race," *Critical Inquiry* 22, no. 4 (1996): 713, 733.

25. Leah Hunt-Hendrix and Astra Taylor, *Solidarity: The Past, Present, and Future of a World-Changing Idea* (New York: Pantheon, 2024), 312.

26. Indigenous Action Media, "Accomplices Not Allies: Abolishing the Ally Industrial Complex," in *Taking Sides: Revolutionary Solidarity and the Poverty of Liberalism*, ed. Cindy Milstein (Oakland: AK Press, 2015), 87.

27. Indigenous Action Media, "Accomplices Not Allies," 88, 93.

28. Joshua Bloom and Waldo E. Martin, *Black Against Empire: The History and Politics of the Black Panther Party* (Berkeley: University of California Press, 2016), 185.

29. Bloom and Martin, *Black Against Empire*, 211.

30. Bloom and Martin, *Black Against Empire*, 195.

31. Gustavo Esteva, "The Oaxaca Commune and Mexico's Coming Insurrection," *Antipode* 42, no. 4 (September 2010): 985, https://doi.org/10.1111/j.1467-8330.2010.00784.x.

32. Barucha Peller, "Self-Reproduction and the Oaxaca Commune," *Roar*, March 18, 2016, https://roarmag.org/magazine/reproducing-the-oaxaca-commune/.

33. M. E. O'Brien, *Family Abolition: Capitalism and the Communizing of Care* (London: Pluto Press, 2023), 206–8.

34. Lynn Stephen, *We Are the Face of Oaxaca: Testimony and Social Movements* (Durham: Duke University Press, 2013), 250.

35. Jessica K. Taft, *The Kids Are in Charge: Activism and Power in Peru's Movement of Working Children* (New York: New York University Press, 2019), 22.

36. Taft, *The Kids Are in Charge*, 102, 107.

37. Taft, *The Kids Are in Charge*, 107, 108.

38. Kay Gabriel, "Inventing the Crisis," *N+1*, April 10, 2024, https://www.nplusonemag.com/issue-47/politics/inventing-the-crisis/.

39. Alva Gotby, *They Call It Love: The Politics of Emotional Life* (London: Verso, 2023), 78.

40. Gotby, *They Call It Love*, 144.

41. Lola Olufemi, *Experiments in Imagining Otherwise* (Maidstone: Hajar Press, 2021), 9.

42. Elisée Reclus, *La Revue blanche: Enquête sur la Commune de Paris*, ed. Jean Baronnet (Paris: Éd. de l'Amateur, 2011), 81–82; as translated in Kristin Ross, *Communal Luxury: The Political Imaginary of the Paris Commune* (London: Verso, 2016), 5.

43. Kristin Ross, *The Politics and Poetics of Everyday Life* (London: Verso, 2023), 291.

44. O'Brien, *Family Abolition*, 231.

45. Anna Feigenbaum et al., *Protest Camps* (London: Zed, 2013), 233.

46. Feigenbaum et al., *Protest Camps*, 183.

47. Le Guin, *The Dispossessed*, xix

About the Author

Photo © Hali Autumn

Madeline Lane-McKinley is a feminist writer, parent, and teacher based in Portland, Oregon. She is the author of *Comedy Against Work: Utopian Longing in Dystopian Times* and *Dear Z*, the coauthor of *Fag/Hag*, and an editor for *Blind Field: A Journal of Cultural Inquiry*. Her writing has appeared in publications such as the *Los Angeles Review of Books*, *Boston Review*, *The New Inquiry*, and *Protean Magazine*.

About Haymarket Books

Haymarket Books is a radical, independent, nonprofit book publisher based in Chicago. Our mission is to publish books that contribute to struggles for social and economic justice. We strive to make our books a vibrant and organic part of social movements and the education and development of a critical, engaged, and internationalist Left.

We take inspiration and courage from our namesakes, the Haymarket Martyrs, who gave their lives fighting for a better world. Their 1886 struggle for the eight-hour day—which gave us May Day, the international workers' holiday—reminds workers around the world that ordinary people can organize and struggle for their own liberation. These struggles—against oppression, exploitation, environmental devastation, and war—continue today across the globe.

Since our founding in 2001, Haymarket has published more than nine hundred titles. Radically independent, we seek to drive a wedge into the risk-averse world of corporate book publishing. Our authors include Angela Y. Davis, Arundhati Roy, Keeanga-Yamahtta Taylor, Eve Ewing, aja monet, Mariame Kaba, Naomi Klein, Rebecca Solnit, Mohammed El-Kurd, José Olivarez, Noam Chomsky, Winona LaDuke, Robyn Maynard, Leanne Betasamosake Simpson, Howard Zinn, Mike Davis, Marc Lamont Hill, Dave Zirin, Astra Taylor, and Amy Goodman, among many other leading writers of our time. We are also the trade publishers of the acclaimed Historical Materialism Book Series.

Haymarket also manages a vibrant community organizing and event space in Chicago, Haymarket House, the popular Haymarket Books Live event series and podcast, and the annual Socialism Conference.

Also Available from Haymarket Books

We Grow the World Together
Parenting Toward Abolition
Edited by Maya Schenwar and Kim Wilson

Care
The Highest Stage of Capitalism
Premilla Nadasen

After Accountability
A Critical Genealogy of a Concept
Pinko Collective

Enemy Feminisms
TERFs, Policewomen, and Girlbosses Against Liberation
Sophie Lewis

Teach Truth
The Struggle for Antiracist Education
Jesse Hagopian

How to End Family Policing
From Outrage to Action
Edited by Erin Miles Cloud, Erica R. Meiners,
Shannon Perez-Darby, and C. Hope Tolliver

Prisons Must Fall
Jane Ball and Mariame Kaba